cocktails

shaken and stirred

DOUGLAS ANKRAH

Cocktails
Shaken and Stirred
by Douglas Ankrah

Photographs by Lisa Linder

Kyle Books

This paperback edition published in 2008
by Kyle Books
An imprint of Kyle Cathie Limited
www.kylecathie.com

Distributed by National Book Network
4501 Forbes Blvd., Suite 200
Lanham, MD 20706
Phone: (301) 459 3366 Fax: (301) 429 5746

Text copyright © 2005 Douglas Ankrah
Photography copyright © 2005 Lisa Linder
except for pp 120, 127, 128–129, 130
Book design © 2005 Kyle Cathie Limited

First published by Kyle Cathie Limited 2004

ISBN: 978-1-904920-79-3

The Library of Congress Cataloging-in-
Publication Data is available on file.

Editor: Sophie Allen
Design and Art Direction: Susanna Cook of
  Allies
Photography: Lisa Linder
Home Economist: Robert Reed
Stylist: Lucinda Maydon
Indexer: Alex Corrin
Production: Sha Huxtable & Alice Holloway

Color reproduction by Scanhouse
Printed and bound by Tien Wah Press,
Singapore

Acknowledgments:

A very special thanks to my mom, Theodora. Thanks
for all your support and for handling me with care. This
book is dedicated to you.

Thanks to Ms Ewa Helwich for all her assistance and
hard work during the photo shoots for the book – the
lady bartender in London...
Robert Reed: your food creations truly match my drink
creations, and for being patient...
Michael and Catherine Mckenna for the jewellery,
Isabella Kristensen for that sexy dress on the front
cover...
All at Kyle Cathie for giving *Shaken & Stirred* a chance
and to Bill Knott...
Big thanks to Graham Syme for all his help over the
years.

Picture Acknowledgments
120 right, Karen Marchant, General Manager of Duke's
Hotel; 127 El Floridita; 128 right, Victor Bergeron,129,
Patrons dining at Trader Vic's, Time Life Pictures/Getty
Images; 130 bond girls. clockwise from top left: Miss
Moneypenny and Bond, Goldfinger; Pussy Galore,
Goldfinger; Bibi Dahl, For Your Eyes Only (ph Keith
Hamshere); Holly Goodhead, Moonraker (ph Patrick
Morin); May Day, A View to a Kill; Jinx, Die Another
Day (ph Keith Hamshere); Tiffany Case, Diamonds are
Forever; Kissy Suzuki, You Only Live Twice; Honey
Rider, Doctor No; Christmas Jones, The World is Not
Enough(ph Keith Hamshere); all Danjaq/Eon/UA,
courtesy of Kobal Collection.

Special thanks to these companies for their generosity
in lending items for the Entertaining at Home section:-
Babylon Design, Ceramica Blue, The Conran Shop,
The Cross, Harrods, Inwater, Liberty, Muji, Musa,
Ozwald Boateng, Paul Smith,Tom McEwan for his
gorgeous jewels (bond girls section), Steiner of
Visionary Living for his fabulous flowers and vases.

All cocktail recipes serve 2 people, unless
stated otherwise.

Contents

Introduction

What is a cocktail? A dictionary might tell you that it is a mixed drink, often iced, flavored, sweetened, and based on a liquor of some kind.

While that might be literally true—and indeed is true of most of the cocktails in this book—a cocktail is much more than that to me. It is creativity, skill, and flair in a glass. It can create a special atmosphere just by being lovingly made and attractively served; even before customers in my bar have taken a sip, I can sometimes feel their mood changing.

It is not simply an alcoholic mish-mash. During Prohibition, it is true that many mixed drinks were made from inferior ingredients, and some cocktails were designed to conceal bathtub gin or some other unspeakable hooch. Nowadays, however, there is no excuse for using inferior liquors: even in the unlikely event that you can disguise them with ice and flavorings, there will be no disguising your hangover the next morning.

This book is the culmination of my experiences of shaking, muddling, mixing, and straining drinks professionally for the last fifteen years. It is not just a handbook for bartenders, however, it is a guide to reproducing at home some of the drinks you would normally find only in smart cocktail bars.

When I create a new cocktail, I often find my inspiration—like, I think, a musician might—from the people and things around me: a song on the radio, the people I meet, the places I visit, the smell of a garden… any stimuli, really, that get the creative juices flowing.

I always try to create drinks that look stunning and taste fantastic—a perfect drink should be the perfect color. I love the mechanics of making a new cocktail, and the theatrical aspect of conjuring up cocktails at the bar, but the biggest kick I get is from a delighted customer.

My aim in writing this book was to demystify the whole process of mixing cocktails; at the same time, I wanted to give a real sense of the fun and energy on which the best bars thrive. This, I hope, is a stylish book to read and enjoy, as well as a friendly, no-nonsense guide to making the best drinks possible.

Some of the cocktails are straightforward, others take a little more skill and patience, but they are all achievable, and if you derive even half the pleasure from mixing them as I have from creating them, then I'll be happy.

Take your time over making cocktails: not so long that the ice melts, but enough to plan carefully what ingredients and equipment you will need. It's easier in a bar because you have all the ingredients to hand, but at home you really have the time to perfect each drink. If you are having a party, just choose two or three drinks that you feel confident making. Think about the garnish: it is often said that people eat with their eyes. I think they drink with them, too.

Experiment, especially once you have mastered the basics. Taste everything you make, even for other people. Is it too strong? Too weak? Too sweet? Too bitter? Many faults can be corrected immediately, with an extra drop or two of sugar syrup, lemon juice, or bitters: if not, at least you will know better next time. Experiment, too, with different fruits: many of the recipes in the book can be altered to suit whatever is available. Much better to make a slightly different drink using fruit that is in season, rather than slavishly follow a recipe using frozen or tinned fruit.

Skill and flair take a little practice, but the creativity is inside you already. Happy shaking, happy stirring, and happy drinking!

Glassware

Hugely important to the success of any cocktail is the right choice of glass. Serve a martini in a highball glass, or a negroni in a martini glass, and you will see what I mean. It just doesn't work.

One thing to bear in mind is the strength of the drink: a long drink made with club soda or cola—a mojito for example—often needs a taller glass than a short, strong drink like an old-fashioned. A small surface area at the top of the drink helps to keep a fizzy drink bubbling; a bigger surface area can help flavors to develop in the glass, as with an old-fashioned. The volume of a drink—the amount of liquid—is also, obviously, important in deciding the correct glass to use.

Some glasses, like the martini glass, are designed for a cold drink without rocks of ice; others, like a highball, are perfect for a gin and tonic. I have recommended a particular glass for each of the cocktails in the book, but if you start to experiment—as I hope you will—with your own drinks, then bear in mind the ideas I've outlined here before you choose which glass to serve them in.

Consider also whether you will serve it with a straw, how the glass will help or hinder the presentation of your cocktail, and—most importantly, because you need to think ahead—whether you want the glass to be frozen: martinis are much better in really cold glasses. Try to keep a few martini glasses and a few shot glasses in the freezer, just in case.

The key glasses used are:-

Highball—a tall glass used for long drinks.

Old-fashioned—a short, sturdy glass ideal for serving scotch on the rocks, or any hard liquor with a small top-up of mixer.

Champagne Flute—currently the most widely used glass for champagne and champagne cocktails.

Shot or Jigger 1$\frac{1}{4}$ oz.—designed for drinks consumed in one go and also for measuring out alcohols for mixed drinks.

Martini 5oz.—a straight-sided classic glass with a long stem to prevent the drink warming up. Best for a classic gin or vodka martini.

Martini 7oz.—good for weaker, fruit-based martinis.

Goblet—large, stemmed glass (a double wine glass) ideal for "fancy" cocktails.

Brandy Balloon—elegant glass usually containing a double measure.

Equipment
Lots of different equipment is available to the cocktail aficionado, but you can make most of the drinks in this book without investing hundreds of dollars in state-of-the-art tools.

One thing you really should invest in, however, is a Boston cocktail shaker, which comes in 2 halves: a toughened glass, which forms a perfect seal, with a stainless steel cup that is slightly wider at the rim, allowing the 2 halves to be sharply rapped together and safely shaken, without redecorating your kitchen in fruit and alcohol.

A coil-rimmed bar strainer is a useful investment: you could use a small mesh strainer to achieve the same results, but the bar strainer fits neatly over the cocktail shaker glass and is perfect for keeping ice out of drinks.

Professional blenders tend to be a little sturdier and have bigger motors than domestic versions, but your home blender will be fine for most blended drinks. Just be careful not to use hard cubed ice: it will not crack properly and may well break the motor. Use crushed ice instead, or pour over rocks after blending.

A mixing glass is used for stirring cocktails with ice—a martini, for example. It tends to be larger than a Boston glass, but either will do.

A good sized ice bucket is also handy, with tongs for hard ice cubes and a small scoop for crushed ice.

Aside from that, the usual bottle openers and corkscrews are handy: the Waiter's (or Barman's) Friend is the simplest and best.

Bar spoons are really just long-handled teaspoons, used for stirring tall glasses or occasionally for light muddling duties: bruising mint leaves, or lime leaves, for instance. It can also be used for layering shooters, or for floats.

Free-pouring is much easier using pourers: they are cork and chrome spouts that fit in the bottle's neck and provide a thin, constant stream of drink. They also help with the theatrical aspect of cocktail making—if that is something that appeals!

A muddler is essential for extracting the juice from fruit, for bruising mint leaves, and bashing other herbs. Most are wooden and look a little like small rolling pins.

Jiggers and double jiggers are useful for measuring the small amounts called for in cocktails and help maintain the right proportions in your drinks. The UK dual measure (pictured) holds 25ml and 50ml but American double jiggers vary, holding 1 oz. and 2 oz. or $^3/_4$ oz. and $1^1/_4$ oz. An American single jigger holds $1^1/_2$ oz.

A fine strainer or tea strainer is useful, especially for drinks with lots of pulp or seeds.

A good, sharp knife and a small chopping board are vital for cleanly prepared, appetizing garnishes.

Methods

Stirring

If you don't have a mixing glass, you can use the cocktail shaker glass. Fill up your mixing glass with ice cubes then add the alcohol and the liqueur, stir with a bar spoon or a dessert spoon. Classic drinks like a martini are made in this way.

Layering

Most layered drinks are made in shot glasses and usually consist of liqueurs as they float better. To layer or float a liquid pour over the back of a barspoon (or a teaspoon) into the glass.

Blending

Blended drinks can be a nightmare to make. If you can, use crushed ice or simply put about 8–10 ice cubes in a large lintfree dishtowel and bash them until evenly crushed. Make sure you use the correct measures so the drinks blend well with the ice. Blend for about 20 seconds and use ripe fruit.

Pouring

When making drinks, make sure you pour the correct amount. Too much alcohol will ruin the drink. Example: when making a gin and tonic, make sure the highball glass is filled with cubed ice then pour in your gin, then the tonic, finally stir it really well, and then garnish.

Shaking

The aim of shaking a cocktail is to make sure that the drink you are planning to serve is both cold and thoroughly mixed. It can also introduce air into the drink, which can give a slightly frothy texture to some cocktails, especially cream-based drinks. A cocktail shaker is made up of 2 pieces, a large heavy glass and its metal counterpart. Pour your ingredients into the ice-filled cocktail shaker glass, as this allows you to see the amount of alcohol and liqueurs you're using for the drink. The stainless steel cocktail shaker "glass" acts as a lid, and is the right volume for 2 drinks. Shake for about 10–15 seconds, enough time to dissolve the sugar into the spirit. The metal of the shaker should be freezing cold by the time you have finished; finally, strain the cocktail and discard the ice.

Muddling

Muddling involves crushing fruit, herbs (usually mint), and sometimes sugar together to create a flavorsome residue. Drinks like the caipirinha and mojito are muddled in a heavy or toughened old-fashioned glass.

Bashing

Usually you bash herbs or some fruits (like watermelon) to break them up and release the flavor. You can use a muddler or rolling pin.

Ice

Just as anyone learning to cook needs to understand what heat does to food, so any aspiring cocktail-maker needs to know how ice affects drinks. Ice is vital both for making and for serving cocktails, and it can make a huge difference to the success of a drink.

When cocktails started being popular again in Britain, a lot of customers, used to the flimsy remnants of ice in the bucket on the bar in their local bar or pub, were surprised at the sheer quantity of ice used by good bartenders. Old-fashioned glasses were filled with rocks of hard ice, highballs were filled to the brim with crushed ice and two myths about ice emerged. The first is that cocktail bars fill glasses with ice because ice is cheap. In any good bar, this is simply untrue. You can ask for less ice in a drink if you like, but that does not mean you will get more of everything else: it simply means your drink will be less successful. Which brings us to myth number two: that the more ice a drink contains, the more dilute it will be. In fact, a glass filled with ice stays much colder than a glass with only a little ice: be stingy with the ice, and it will simply melt into the drink.

An iced cocktail should still have plenty of ice in the glass when the drink has been finished: if it doesn't, it should either have had more (or colder) ice to start with, or it should have been drunk more quickly.

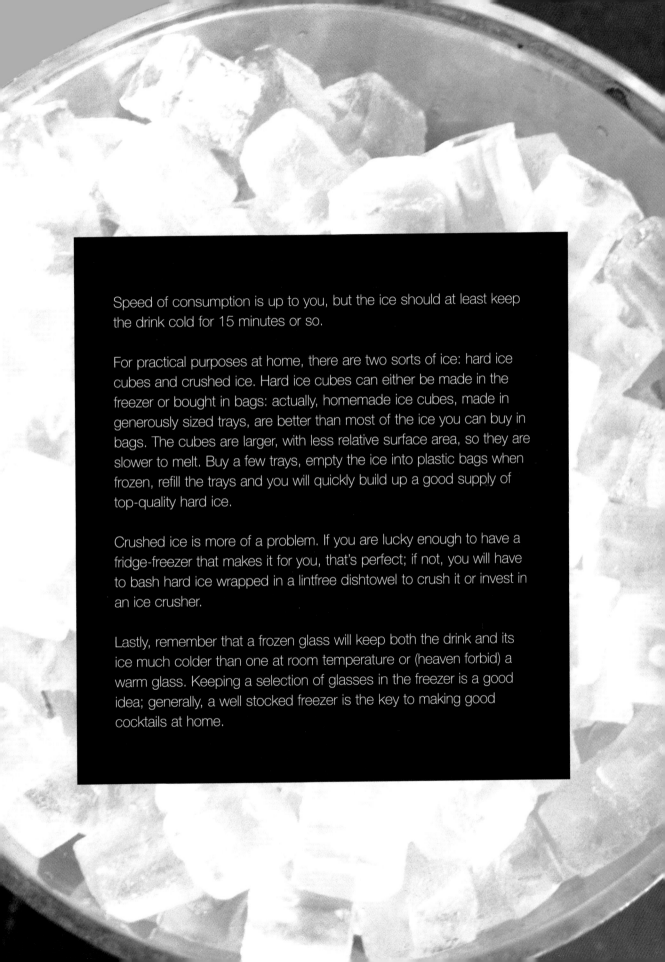

Speed of consumption is up to you, but the ice should at least keep the drink cold for 15 minutes or so.

For practical purposes at home, there are two sorts of ice: hard ice cubes and crushed ice. Hard ice cubes can either be made in the freezer or bought in bags: actually, homemade ice cubes, made in generously sized trays, are better than most of the ice you can buy in bags. The cubes are larger, with less relative surface area, so they are slower to melt. Buy a few trays, empty the ice into plastic bags when frozen, refill the trays and you will quickly build up a good supply of top-quality hard ice.

Crushed ice is more of a problem. If you are lucky enough to have a fridge-freezer that makes it for you, that's perfect; if not, you will have to bash hard ice wrapped in a lintfree dishtowel to crush it or invest in an ice crusher.

Lastly, remember that a frozen glass will keep both the drink and its ice much colder than one at room temperature or (heaven forbid) a warm glass. Keeping a selection of glasses in the freezer is a good idea; generally, a well stocked freezer is the key to making good cocktails at home.

Garnishing

Fashion in garnishing drinks changes almost as often as fashions in ladies' hats; in fact, in the 30s, hats and cocktails looked rather similar.

The classic garnishes—the olive in a martini or the cherry in a Manhattan—are really part of the drink: small, reasonably discreet, and rather elegant, adding a complementary or contrasting flavor or aroma to the cocktail.

From the 70s, however, drinks started to change. Pina coladas and tequila sunrises started to be served with theatrical pizazz in hollowed-out coconuts or pineapples, overwhelmed with exotic fruit, gaudily colored mini-umbrellas and sparklers until the drink itself was barely noticeable.

Such pyrotechnic miracles of the bartender's art are still available in various corners of the globe, mostly next to swimming pools in tropical holiday resorts, but elsewhere a more restrained approach has taken hold.

The point of a garnish is to enhance the drink, not to overwhelm it. As with food, the idea is both to please the eye and to give the palate an idea of what to expect. Why chefs ever thought that a scratchy sprig of parsley made their creation more attractive is difficult to understand; similarly, a moribund lemon slice or a gratuitous cherry adds nothing to a drink.

Use your imagination too! If you are making a drink with elderflower syrup, for example, and you have elderflowers in the garden, then use them, or perhaps try a fresh bay leaf in a martini. Cocktail bars do not, as a rule, have herb or fruit gardens, so make the most of your advantage and personalise your drinks.

When a recipe calls for, say, a dozen raspberries, make sure you save the best examples to top the drink; similarly, mint bashed in a mojito does not have to be of pristine quality, but the sprig on top should be fresh and bright green.

A sharp knife and a good little chopping board are essential for garnishes: sharp, clean cuts look attractive and help to stop garnishes from discoloring.

These are the best ways of garnishing cocktails:

Lemon and lime wedges—top and tail, cut in half lengthwise and then cut each half into 3–4 wedges, depending on size. Choose attractive fruit with evenly colored skin for garnishing; less beautiful examples can be used for juicing.

Lemon, lime, and orange twists—these are long strips of zest; the idea is to make use of the citrus oils in the skin, which give an inimitable aroma to drinks. The pith, by contrast, is bitter and needs to be trimmed off. Top and tail the fruit, then carefully pare a strip from the skin all the way from top to bottom—about ½-inch wide for an orange, ¼-inch for a lemon and a little less for a lime. Turn it pith-side up on a cutting board and, holding it with thumb and forefinger, carefully saw away the pith until you can see just the color of the fruit. The twist will now add flavor from both sides, with no bitterness.

Lemon, lime, and kiwi fruit wheels—use the best examples you can find and slice across the widest part of the fruit into rounds, about ¼-inch wide. You can then cut from the peel to the center so that the wheel will perch easily on the rim of a glass.

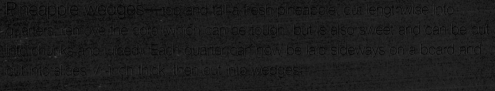

Pineapple wedges—top and tail a fresh pineapple, cut lengthwise into quarters, remove the core (which can be tough, but is also sweet and can be cut into chunks and juiced). Each quarter can now be laid sideways on a board and cut into slices ½-inch thick, then cut into wedges.

Pineapple leaves—just pick a few of the best-looking leaves off the top of a pineapple and slide them onto the rim of the glass.

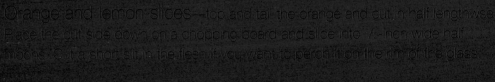

Orange and lemon slices—top and tail the orange and cut in half lengthwise. Place the cut side down on a chopping board and slice into ¼-inch-wide half moons. Cut a short slit in the flesh if you want to perch it on the rim of the glass.

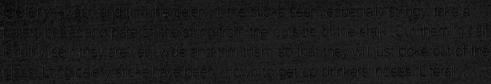

Celery—wash and trim the celery; if the sticks seem especially stringy, take a potato peeler and pare off the string from the outside of the stalk. Cut them in half lengthwise if they are very wide and trim them so that they will just poke out of the glass. Long celery sticks have been known to get up drinkers' noses. Literally.

Olives—a wide variety of olives can be found in delis and supermarkets: green, black, dried black, Kalamata, and stuffed green, to name a few. For cocktails, large unstuffed, pitted green olives are the classic, but you might experiment with pimento-, almond-, or even anchovy-stuffed green olives.

Maraschino cherries—you either love them or hate them, but they have a strong, sweet almond/cherry flavor and should be used with discretion.

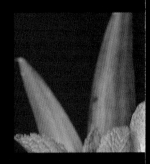

Pearl onions—the classic garnish which turns a martini into a Gibson: 2 pearl onions speared on a cocktail stick. A dash of the vinegary juice makes a martini a dirty martini.

Strawberries—the bigger and more beautiful the better for garnishing: use any slightly squashy, small, or unattractive specimens for juicing or muddling. Leave on the green leafy top if it looks good and carefully slit the bottom of the berry so it can cling to the rim.

Mint—fresh green mint is really important, for flavor as well as looks. Look for springy bunches with thin red stalks and a bright, pale-green color; even better, grow it in your garden—it is a very hardy little herb.

Banana slices—slice the banana diagonally into 1/2-inch thick slices, rub with a little lemon juice and slit from skin to center to hold it to the rim of a glass. Leaving the skin on is sensible.

Cucumber slices—leave the skin on for garnishing a Pimm's, peel it for a paler drink and slice straight across or diagonally, according to aesthetic taste and the size of your cucumber. Slices should be about 1/4-inch wide.

Apple fans—cut a section from one side of a crisp green or red apple, lay it flat on a board, slice off both ends and then cut into 5 or 6 neat, thin slices. Carefully skewer all the slices at one end with a toothpick, then fan out into a sort of Sydney Opera House arrangement and dust with a mixture of confectioners' sugar and ground cinnamon. You can also make pear fans, lemon fans, strawberry fans, and mango fans.

Lemongrass tubes—cut the lemongrass about a third of the way up. Open out the layers and they should naturally curve back into little tubes that you insert into the drink.

Straws—obviously these are used for drinking the cocktail, but they can also be used as a garnish and to mix the drink.

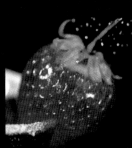

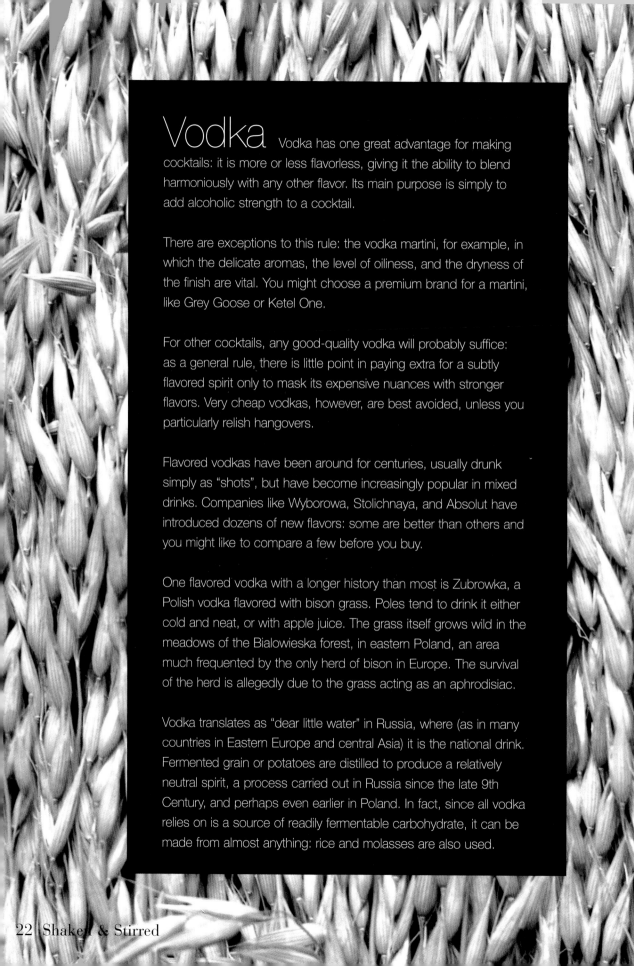

Vodka

Vodka has one great advantage for making cocktails: it is more or less flavorless, giving it the ability to blend harmoniously with any other flavor. Its main purpose is simply to add alcoholic strength to a cocktail.

There are exceptions to this rule: the vodka martini, for example, in which the delicate aromas, the level of oiliness, and the dryness of the finish are vital. You might choose a premium brand for a martini, like Grey Goose or Ketel One.

For other cocktails, any good-quality vodka will probably suffice: as a general rule, there is little point in paying extra for a subtly flavored spirit only to mask its expensive nuances with stronger flavors. Very cheap vodkas, however, are best avoided, unless you particularly relish hangovers.

Flavored vodkas have been around for centuries, usually drunk simply as "shots", but have become increasingly popular in mixed drinks. Companies like Wyborowa, Stolichnaya, and Absolut have introduced dozens of new flavors: some are better than others and you might like to compare a few before you buy.

One flavored vodka with a longer history than most is Zubrowka, a Polish vodka flavored with bison grass. Poles tend to drink it either cold and neat, or with apple juice. The grass itself grows wild in the meadows of the Bialowieska forest, in eastern Poland, an area much frequented by the only herd of bison in Europe. The survival of the herd is allegedly due to the grass acting as an aphrodisiac.

Vodka translates as "dear little water" in Russia, where (as in many countries in Eastern Europe and central Asia) it is the national drink. Fermented grain or potatoes are distilled to produce a relatively neutral spirit, a process carried out in Russia since the late 9th Century, and perhaps even earlier in Poland. In fact, since all vodka relies on is a source of readily fermentable carbohydrate, it can be made from almost anything: rice and molasses are also used.

Gin

Gin has a long and somewhat chequered history. The classic flavoring is dried juniper berries and most sources seem to think that the Dutch (who still drink various kinds of jenever) invented it, although the Italians also have a claim, perhaps because Italy has traditionally been the source for juniper.

The only gin worth buying is one in which the "gin head" is employed: a method of distilling the spirit with the botanicals to create subtle and well balanced flavors. Cheaper and cruder methods simply involve adding flavorings, or macerating the spirit with botanicals. None of the well-known brands employs these techniques, although dubiously labeled gins made in Asia or Africa almost certainly do.

Like many spirits and liqueurs, gin started life as a medicine, with claims made for its efficacy in treating dozens of complaints, ranging from gout to gallstones. By the 18th Century, however, the popularity of cheap, badly distilled gin in London and other cities had led to the sort of social breakdown famously lampooned by Hogarth in his etching "Gin Lane". Distribution was controlled, taxes were raised, and the English went back to beer.

Two styles of gin are officially recognized: London and Plymouth, differing mainly in the botanicals employed in their manufacture. London gin tends to favor juniper while, in Plymouth gin, orris root is a dominant aroma. Other gins are now available with a variety of not-so-traditional flavorings: try Hendrick's gin, flavored with cucumber and rose petals, or Tanqueray No.10, which employs fresh botanicals in the gin head instead of the usual dried herbs, roots, and spices.

Strength is an important factor with gin: alcohol content ranges from 37.5% alcohol for Gordon's to 47.3% for Tanqueray No.10, a vital consideration when mixing a martini. Lower strength gins might be better straight from the freezer, higher strength gins stirred with ice, but it really depends on personal preference. You may well find that your favorite brand of gin for a martini is different from your favorite to mix with tonic. Happy experiments, however, are assured.

Tequila

Before Cortes and his Spanish conquistadores toppled the Aztec kingdom in Mexico, locals had grown rather fond of a milky, slightly sour cactus "beer" called pulque.

While pulquerias still survive in Mexico, the technology that the Spanish brought with them allowed them to distill pulque into a spirit, known as tequila and now Mexico's national drink. Tequila is actually a sort of mezcal, with production restricted to the Jalisco region around Guadalajara and the town Tequila, where the best variety of blue agave cactus thrives.

As with any spirit, what comes out of the still is a clear liquid at high proof. It can then either be bottled as it is, darkened with caramel to give an illusion of age (often called simply "gold"), or actually aged in wood, which mellows the spirit and adds notes of vanilla and other spices to the drink: añejo and reposado are the two terms which guarantee a wood-aged tequila.

Its assertive flavor is difficult, but not impossible, to balance in cocktails, which is perhaps why the classic methods of shots and slammers are most popular. Mexicans themselves tend to use salt, chile, and lime to accompany cheaper versions, but a really good barrel-aged tequila can be sipped like malt whisky or a fine dark rum.

Rum

Chemically speaking, sugar cane is the easiest and most efficient crop to ferment and then distill and countries in which sugar cane grows have taken full advantage of the fact. Rum is made all over the Caribbean and Central America.

Rum's history is inextricably and romantically linked with pirates, buccaneering on the high seas and tots of grog, and less happily with the slave trade. The sugar cane plantations originally used slave labor, and slaves were regularly traded for rum.

Either the juice or the molasses from sugar cane is fermented to produce a clear spirit, then, as with tequila, the result can either be bottled as white rum, or aged, often with caramel or molasses added to intensify color.

Both Bacardi and Havana Club produce a range of rums from white to dark and wood-aged: white rum is perhaps best suited to a mojito, its young and powerful flavor ideally matched with mint, lime, and sugar, while the rich aroma and flavor of darker rums are better suited to mellower combinations: soft summer fruits, for example. The best rums need nothing but a snifter, especially the artisanal rums from Martinique (look for the word "Agricole") and Haiti.

Wray & Nephew rum from Jamaica is reputed to have medicinal properties: local people use it as a cure for headaches or flu. The method involves applying a rum-soaked cloth to the forehead, although drinking it may prove equally efficacious.

Scotch whisky

The Scottish may not have been the first to make whisky—that distinction probably belongs to the Irish—but Scotch whisky is now the most famous and widely available spirit in the world.

The best Scotch is made from malted barley, roasted over a peat fire, fermented, then distilled in a pot still, and aged in wood for 8 years or more, when it can be sold as "single malt". Cheaper Scotch uses a proportion of lighter flavored grain whisky in a blend with malt whisky, hence the term "blended".

Some blended whiskies, however, are perfect for cocktails—J&B Rare is a good example—whereas the distinctively peaty malts from Islay—Lagavulin, for instance—are best drunk on their own; indeed, making a whisky sour with Islay malt is probably a hanging offence in the Western Isles of Scotland.

All Scotch is, to a greater or lesser extent, peaty, since at least some of the malt is roasted in an open kiln: in Ireland, the kiln is closed, so Irish whiskey (with an 'e') is traditionally unpeaty. The Irish also distill three times rather than twice, in theory making a smoother drink. Any cocktail specifying Scotch can be made equally successfully with Irish whiskey.

The huge international popularity of Scotch whisky has led many countries to make their own, with varying results: the best, surprisingly, are the Japanese, whose Suntory whiskeys are very well made. The latest entrant in the international whisky stakes is India: Amrut whisky is made with malt grown in the foothills of the Himalayas and distilled in Bangalore. The optimistic distillers plan to sell it, amongst other places, in Scottish curry houses.

Bourbon

Despite its all-American image, Bourbon actually owes its existence to Scottish whisky makers: a group of immigrant Scots started making whisky in Kentucky in the 18th Century using maize, a crop better suited to local conditions than the barley they had used at home.

Bourbon is instantly identifiable as different from malt whisky; the corn gives a sweetness to the nose and palate, while the charred oak barrels used for maturation give it a smoky aroma and strong hints of vanilla.

At its best, bourbon stands comparison with the finest single malts, especially single batch bourbons, often bottled at cask strength. Less rarified bourbons—Maker's Mark and Woodford Reserve, for instance—are perfect for cocktails, with pronounced flavors that marry well with orange zest, summer fruits, and warm spices. The vanilla component in bourbon can be easily enhanced by inserting a slit vanilla bean into the bottle.

Jack Daniel's, a very similar whiskey to bourbon, is actually from neighbouring Tennessee and is known as "Tennessee Sour Mash"; it can be used in any cocktail recipe that specifies bourbon.

Stocking the Bar
The cocktail kitchen has much in common with any kitchen: it relies on fresh ingredients, especially fruit, but it also needs a stock of basics.

We have already discussed spirits that are essential for your bar stock and, by making some of the cocktails in this book, you will gradually accumulate a stock of liqueurs. As well as these, however, you might find the following list useful.

Vermouth—red (sweet) and white (dry) vermouths are indispensable in a whole host of cocktails. Vya, from California, and Noilly Prat, from France, are the two most famous premium brands. Both make both red and white, although the Noilly Prat red can be hard to find. Martini Extra Dry and Martini Rosso are widely available.

Bitters—Angostura bitters are essential: if you are a fan of bitters-flavored drinks, you might want to invest in bottles of orange or peach bitters.
Worcestershire sauce is vital for a Bloody Mary, or any tomato-based cocktail, as is Tabasco.

Garnishes—jars of maraschino cherries, olives, and pearl onions are easy to store in the fridge or the cupboard. Fruit garnishes need to be fresh, and should be bought as needed, but keeping a few lemons and limes in the refrigerator or fruitbowl is a good idea if you need an emergency cocktail. Supermarkets often sell fruit when it is not yet ripe, so it is often best to buy fresh fruit a couple of days before you want to use it so you can ripen it properly—this will improve your cocktails no end.

Sugar Syrup—simple syrup—features in many of the recipes in this book. It has the advantage of already being dissolved, so it can be stirred or shaken into a drink very easily. To make your own, heat 2 1/2 cups of water, and once it is boiling add 5 1/2 cups (2 1/4 lb.) sugar, and boil until it becomes a thick syrup—about 10–15 minutes. Add more water if it becomes too thick. Remove any scum from the top, let cool, and funnel into clean bottles. Otherwise, buy it from any good cocktail-friendly liquor store.

Sugars—the other sugars it helps to have are superfine and soft brown sugar, both cheap and easy to find, and vanilla sugar, which can either be bought, or made at home. To make it blend 3 fresh vanilla pods with 5 1/2 cups (2 1/4 lb.) sugar. Once blended, sift to catch some of the larger black pieces. Store in an airtight container.

Juices and sodas—juices are best made or bought fresh: in any case, long-life juices rarely make a good drink. An exception is cranberry juice, which is usually long-life and actually a "juice drink", with water and added sugar. Also, good-quality canned or long-life tomato juice can make a decent Bloody Mary.

Honey—acacia or any runny honey are best—is useful, as is a good espresso coffee, celery salt, and cans or packets of coconut cream. Ground cinnamon and whole nutmeg also come in handy for dusting over garnishes or creamy drinks.

Tonic water, soda water, lemonade (7-Up for preference), and ginger beer (Fentiman's is best) are always useful: try to find cans, rather than huge bottles. It may work out a little more expensive, but nothing dulls a drink more than flat tonic or soda water.

Fruit purees—specialist stores now sell a good range of frozen fruit purees, which are excellent for cocktails. What you want to stock in your freezer will depend on your favorite drinks: Bellini fans will look for frozen peach puree, while aficionados of the fruity martini might go for passionfruit, raspberries, or blackberries.
You can, of course, make your own: almost any berry can be cooked with a little sugar, pureed, strained, and frozen in ice cube trays. Here are recipes for passionfruit and raspberry.

Passionfruit puree

14 ripe passionfruit
$1^1/4$ cups water
$2^1/2$ cups superfine sugar
Scoop the flesh out of the passionfruit and blend. Boil the water and then add the sugar and passionfruit until the mixture becomes a thick syrup—about 10–15 minutes. Strain and let cool, then either bottle and store in the refrigerator or put it in a bag in the freezer.

Raspberry puree

2 cartons fresh raspberries
$1/2$ cup sugar syrup
Blend the raspberries with the sugar syrup. Push through a fine mesh strainer so that the puree is smooth.

Flavored vodkas—if you don't want to splash out on flavored vodkas, it is easy to make your own. The most useful is raspberry flavored vodka, which is easy to make and gives the bland taste of vodka a delicious twist.

Raspberry flavored vodka

Insert 12 fresh raspberries to a nearly full bottle of vodka, and 1 tablespoon of sugar syrup, and leave for 4–5 days. Strain to remove the raspberries, otherwise they will ferment and ruin the flavor. Store in the refrigerator or freezer.

Vanilla flavored vodka

Split 2 fresh vanilla pods into 2, then insert the pods into a nearly full bottle of vodka. Add $1/4$ cup of sugar syrup and leave for about 4–5 days. Strain and store in the refrigerator or freezer.

Breezes, Collinses, and Martinis

The Breeze

The sea breeze (page 32) is a favorite with bartenders, because it is so quick and easy to make.
At home, it's a perfect party drink: you don't really want to be shaking martinis for 24 people. Try one of the variations on the theme for a more original crowd-pleaser.

The Collins

These days, the collins is perhaps best known as a forerunner of the mojito, which is really just a collins made with rum. However you drink it, a collins is the perfect drink before lunch on a sunny day. For the collins' variations you can use gin or vodka.

The New Martini

The purist will tell you—quite rightly—that just because a drink is in a martini glass doesn't make it a martini. Strictly speaking, a martini is made with gin, not vodka (which makes a vodkatini), and is flavored with just a dash of vermouth.

Rules are made to be broken, however, and a new generation of martinis has sprung up, mostly flavored with fresh fruit and with much less of a kick than the traditional versions.
Four of any of these, and Dorothy Parker might just have avoided ending up under the host.

Summer Breeze

A sort of distillation of the English summer.

2 highball glasses

4 oz. (2½ jiggers) Grey Goose orange vodka (or Absolut Mandrin)
1 oz. (¾ jigger or 2 tablespoons) elderflower syrup
4 oz. (½ cup) cloudy apple juice
4 oz. (½ cup) cranberry juice
hard ice cubes

Garnish: sprigs of mint or apple fans

Method:
Fill the glasses with ice. Pour in the vodka, elderflower syrup, and the juices, stir, and garnish with a sprig of mint or an apple fan.

Sea Breeze

The classic sea breeze is a gentle, easy drinking example of the "strong, sweet, sour, and weak" principle of cocktails, and is a favorite with drinkers all over the world.

2 highball glasses

4 oz. (2½ jiggers) vodka, try Smirnoff Penka
4 oz. (½ cup) cranberry juice
4 oz. (½ cup) pink grapefruit juice
hard ice cubes

Garnish: lime wedges

Method:
Fill the glasses with ice, add the vodka and the rest of the juices, and garnish with a wedge of lime.

Orange Breeze

Making your own orange vodka is easy: dry out the peeled zest of 2 oranges in a very slow oven, or on a radiator, then feed them into a nearly full bottle of vodka, add $3/4$ ounce ($1/2$ jigger) of sugar syrup, shake, and leave for a few days.

2 highball glasses

4 oz. ($2^1/_2$ jiggers) Grey Goose orange vodka (or your homemade orange vodka)
5 oz. (a generous $1/2$ cup) cloudy apple juice
4 oz. ($1/2$ cup) cranberry juice
hard ice cubes

Garnish: orange slices

Method:
Fill the glasses with ice, pour in the vodka and the juices, stir, and garnish with orange slices.

Bay Breeze

The sea breeze's laid-back, tropical cousin, and a perfect drink for the beach.

2 highball glasses

4 oz. ($2^1/_2$ jiggers) Wyborowa pineapple vodka
5 oz. (a generous $1/2$ cup) cranberry juice
4 oz. ($1/2$ cup) fresh pineapple juice
hard ice cubes

Garnish: pineapple slices

Method:
Fill the glasses with ice, pour in the drinks, and stir. Garnish with a thin slice of pineapple.

Melon Breeze

Simple and very refreshing.

2 highball glasses

4 oz. ($2^1/_2$ jiggers) Wyborowa melon vodka
5 oz. (a generous $^1/_2$ cup) cloudy apple juice
4 oz. ($^1/_2$ cup) cranberry juice
hard ice cubes

Garnish: melon slices, with the skin left on

Method:
Fill the glasses with ice, pour in the vodka and the juices, stir, and garnish with a melon slice.

Jamaican Breeze

A terrific summer drink, invented by one of the LAB barstaff, and a good alternative to Pimm's.

2 highball glasses

$3^1/_2$ oz. (2 jiggers) Sailor Jerry Spiced Caribbean rum or Morgan Spiced rum
1 oz. ($^3/_4$ jigger) vanilla liqueur
juice of 1 lime
6 oz. ($^3/_4$ cup) cloudy apple juice
hard ice cubes

Garnish: apple fans

Method:
Fill the glasses with ice. Shake all the ingredients in a cocktail shaker and then pour them over the ice and garnish with an apple fan.

Passionfruit Collins

If you don't want to use sugar syrup, you can make your own passionfruit puree (see page 29) and add it instead.

2 highball glasses

4 oz. (2$\frac{1}{2}$ jiggers) vodka or gin
2 oz. ($\frac{1}{4}$ cup) lemon juice
flesh and seeds of 2 ripe passionfruit
1$\frac{1}{2}$ tablespoons sugar syrup
club soda (to top up)
crushed ice

Garnish: edible flowers and mint leaves

Method:
Half fill a cocktail glass with crushed ice, and add the vodka or gin, lemon juice, passionfruit, and sugar syrup. Stir well and split between the glasses. Top up with more ice almost to the rim, then with soda water. Garnish with a flower and a few mint leaves.

Tom Collins

Nobody is quite sure who Mr Collins was, or even if he existed, but the first version is traditionally said to have been made with "Old Tom", a once-popular sweetened London gin.

2 highball glasses

4 oz. (2$\frac{1}{2}$ jiggers) gin
2 oz. ($\frac{1}{4}$ cup) fresh lemon juice
2 tablespoons sugar syrup
club soda (to top up)
crushed ice

Garnish: lemon twists and sprigs of mint

Method:
Half fill a cocktail shaker with crushed ice, add the gin, lemon juice, and sugar syrup, stir, and split between the glasses. Top up with more ice almost to the rim, then with soda water. Garnish with lemon twists and mint.

Kiwi Fruit Collins

A great looking drink.

2 highball glasses

1 peeled and cubed ripe kiwi fruit
1$^1/_2$ tablespoons sugar syrup
4 oz. (2$^1/_2$ jiggers) vodka
2 oz. ($^1/_4$ cup) lemon juice
club soda or 7-Up (to top up)
crushed ice

Garnish: kiwi fruit wheels

Method:
Muddle the kiwi fruit in a cocktail shaker glass with the sugar syrup and a little crushed ice. Half fill the glass with ice. Add the vodka and lemon juice, stir, and split between the glasses. Top up with more ice almost to the rim, then with soda water or 7-Up, and garnish with kiwi fruit wheels.

Elderflower Collins

If you have some elderflowers to hand, they will make a perfect garnish.

2 highball glasses

4 oz. (2$^1/_2$ jiggers) gin
2 oz. ($^1/_4$ cup) lemon juice
2 tablespoons elderflower syrup
1$^1/_2$ tablespoons sugar syrup
club soda (to top up)
crushed ice

Garnish: elderflowers (optional)

Method:
Half fill a cocktail shaker glass with crushed ice, add the gin, lemon juice, elderflower syrup, and sugar syrup, stir and split between the glasses. Top up with more ice almost to the rim, then with soda water.

Lemongrass Collins

To make your lemongrass vodka, bruise a stalk of lemongrass until soft and push it into a nearly full bottle of vodka. Leave for 3–4 days, shaking occasionally.

2 highball glasses

3 oz. (1^3/$_4$ jiggers) lemongrass-infused vodka
1^1/$_2$ tablespoons sugar syrup
2 oz. (^{1}/$_4$ cup) lemon juice
club soda or 7-up (to top up)
crushed ice

Garnish: lemongrass tubes, mint leaves, and orange twists

Method:
Fill the glasses half way up with crushed ice. Add your vodka, sugar syrup, and lemon juice, and stir until well mixed. Top with more ice almost to the rim, then with club soda or 7-Up, and garnish.

Raspberry Collins

Chambord is a raspberry and blackberry liqueur from the Loire Valley in France. Instead of the Stolichnaya Razberi vodka, you can use homemade raspberry vodka (see page 29).

2 highball glasses

14 raspberries
1^1/$_2$ tablespoons sugar syrup
4 oz. (2^1/$_2$ jiggers) Stolichnaya Razberi vodka
1 oz. (^{3}/$_4$ jigger) Chambord
2 oz. (^{1}/$_4$ cup) lemon juice
soda or 7-Up (to top up)
crushed ice

Garnish: raspberries

Method:
Muddle the raspberries in a cocktail shaker glass with the sugar syrup and a little crushed ice. Half fill the glass with ice. Add the vodka, Chambord, and lemon juice, stir, and split between the glasses. Top up with more ice almost to the rim, then with club soda or 7-Up, and garnish with 2 raspberries.

Lemongrass and Wild Chili Martini

As with the lemongrass collins, you will need to make your own flavored vodka. Bruise 2 stalks of lemongrass gently with a rolling pin, then stick them into a nearly full bottle of vodka with 2 tablespoons of sugar syrup and a red chili which you have pricked all over with a fork. Screw the top back on, shake it gently, then leave the bottle for a week to let the flavors develop, shaking it, when you remember, to help things along. This is an ideal drink for a cold winter's evening.

2 martini glasses, preferably frozen

4 oz. (2$^1/_2$ jiggers) lemongrass and chili vodka
1 oz. ($^3/_4$ jigger) Manzana apple liqueur
2 oz. ($^1/_4$ cup) cloudy apple juice
juice $^1/_2$ lemon
2 tablespoons sugar syrup
hard ice cubes

Garnish: small red chilies and lemongrass tubes

Method:
Put all the ingredients into a cocktail shaker and shake hard. Fine-strain into the glasses and garnish with lemongrass tubes and small, red chili halves.

French Martini

This was very popular in the early 90s at the start of the cocktail revolution. It is a very elegant drink.

2 martini glasses, preferably frozen

3 oz. (1$^3/_4$ jiggers) Finlandia vodka
1 oz. ($^3/_4$ jigger) Chambord (raspberry and blackberry liqueur)
12 raspberries
1$^1/_2$ tablespoons fresh pineapple juice
2 teaspoons sugar syrup
hard ice cubes

Garnish: raspberries

Method:
Shake everything together in a cocktail shaker, then fine-strain into the glasses.
Garnish with raspberries.

Pomegranate Martini

A delicious drink for the pomegranate season.

2 martini glasses, preferably frozen

4 oz. (2$\frac{1}{2}$ jiggers) Finlandia vodka
juice of 2 ripe pomegranates, seeds retained
1$\frac{1}{2}$ tablespoons liquid from a jar of maraschino cherries
8 mint leaves
hard ice cubes

Garnish: pomegranate seeds

Method:
Squeeze the juice out of the pomegranates and retain a few of the seeds for the garnish.
Shake all the ingredients together in a cocktail shaker. Strain into the glasses and garnish with
the seeds.

Raspberry Martini

Vibrantly colored, sensational tasting, and keeps you coming back for more.

2 martini glasses, preferably frozen

12 raspberries
2 oz. (1$\frac{1}{4}$ jiggers) Chambord (raspberry and blackberry liqueur)
4 oz. vodka (2$\frac{1}{2}$ jiggers) Stolichnaya Razberi, or homemade raspberry flavored vodka—
  see page 29
hard ice cubes

Garnish: raspberries

Method:
Muddle the raspberries with the Chambord. Add the vodka and ice, then shake in a cocktail
shaker and fine-strain into the glasses. Garnish with a few raspberries.

Black Star Liner Martini

Named after a shipping line in Ghana, where my family comes from. It was set up many years ago by the Jamaican activist and visionary Marcus Garvey—hardly the last word in opulence nowadays but I think it deserves its own cocktail!

Patrón XO Café is a Mexican coffee-flavored tequila.

2 martini glasses, preferably frozen

1½ oz. (1 jigger) Mozart Chocolate liqueur
1½ oz. (1 jigger) freshly made espresso
1½ oz. (1 jigger) Patrón XO Café
2 teaspoons sugar syrup
hard ice cubes

Garnish: espresso beans and chocolate shavings

Method:
Shake all the ingredients in a cocktail shaker and then strain into the glasses. Add a few whole espresso beans and float chocolate shavings on the top.

Basil and Pineapple Martini

I have used basil and strawberry before but then I saw a bartender using the combination of basil and pineapple and decided to experiment myself. Smirnoff Penka is a great new vodka, with a bottle cap that is ideal for measuring.

2 martini glasses, preferably frozen

1 cup chopped pineapple, cubed
1½ tablespoons sugar syrup
12 basil leaves
4 oz. (2½ jiggers) Smirnoff Penka vodka
1 tablespoon lemon juice
hard ice cubes

Method:
Muddle the pineapple with the basil and sugar syrup in a cocktail glass, then add the vodka, lemon juice, and ice. Shake, then fine-strain into the glasses.

Maverick Martini or Porn Star Martini

Named after a louche Cape Town night club I frequented while writing this book. The shot of champagne on the side of the beautifully colored passionfruit and vanilla martini makes this a very seductive drink. The first time I made these in Townhouse the whole bar was ordering them by the end of the night.

2 martini glasses, preferably frozen, and tall shot glasses for champagne on the side

3 oz. (1³/₄ jiggers) Cariel Vanilla Vodka
1 tablespoon Passoa (passionfruit liqueur)
flesh and seeds of 4 passionfruit
5 teaspoons vanilla sugar
4 oz. (2¹/₂ jiggers) champagne
1 passionfruit, cut in half
hard ice cubes

Method:
Shake all the ingredients except the champagne, the passionfruit halves, and 1 teaspoon of vanilla sugar in a cocktail shaker, and then strain into the glasses. Separately, pour out 2 glasses of champagne and dust the halved passionfruit with the remaining sugar. Dunk the passionfruit in the martini glasses, with spoons: the idea is to fish out the fruit, eat it with the spoon, drink the champagne, and then enjoy the cocktail at leisure.

Blanc Martini

This was on the original menu at LAB the first year it opened. It is a great drink and easy to make at home.

2 martini glasses, preferably frozen

3 oz. (1³/₄ jiggers) Finlandia vodka
1 oz. (³/₄ jigger) white crème de cacao
1 tablespoon coconut cream (Coco Lopez)
2 oz. (¹/₄ cup) single cream
hard ice cubes

Garnish: coconut flakes

Method:
Shake all the ingredients in a cocktail shaker and strain into glasses. Garnish with coconut flakes.

Watermelon Martini

This is at present the darling of the London cocktail scene. A must-have at Townhouse.

2 martini glasses, preferably frozen

6 chunks of watermelon, about 1-inch cubes
2 tablespoons sugar syrup
4 oz. (2¹⁄₂ jiggers) Finlandia vodka
hard ice cubes

Garnish: watermelon slices, with the skin left on

Method:
Bash the watermelon with the sugar syrup in a cocktail shaker glass, and add the ice and vodka. Shake and then fine-strain into the glasses. Serve, garnished with a watermelon slice on the rim of the glass.

Elderflower Martini

Ciroc vodka is a grape-based vodka from France. I used it because it was new to the market and a bit obscure. It is a very unusual tasting vodka and the grape and elderflower work well together. If you don't have Ciroc, you could add a couple of grapes to 1¹⁄₂ ounces (1 jigger) vodka and shake it in a cocktail shaker; otherwise just use good vodka.

2 martini glasses, preferably frozen

2 oz. (1¹⁄₄ jiggers) Ciroc vodka
2 oz. (1¹⁄₄ jiggers) Tanqueray no.10 gin
2 tablespoons sugar syrup
3 tablespoons fresh lemon juice
2 teaspoons grated fresh ginger
2 tablespoons elderflower syrup
hard ice cubes

Method:
Shake all the ingredients in a cocktail shaker, then fine-strain into the glasses.

Passionfruit Martini

Passoa is a coral-red passionfruit liqueur made by Cointreau in Spain. It has a fresh scent of passionfruit and citrus.

2 martini glasses, preferably frozen

4 oz. (2$\frac{1}{2}$ jiggers) Finlandia or Ketel One vodka
flesh and seeds of 4 ripe passionfruit
1 oz. ($\frac{3}{4}$ jigger) Passoa (optional)
hard ice cubes

Garnish: passionfruit halves dusted with confectioners' sugar.

Method:
Shake all the ingredients together in a cocktail shaker and fine-strain into the glasses. Garnish with half a passionfruit.

Morris Major

A frosty version of a hot toddy, shaken, not stirred, to distribute the honey evenly. Named after a legendary Cape Town socialite and bon viveur. For vanilla-infused bourbon, split 2 fresh vanilla beans in half and insert into a nearly full bottle of bourbon and leave for 4–5 days.

2 martini glasses, preferably frozen

4 oz. (2$\frac{1}{2}$ jiggers) vanilla-infused bourbon
2 tablespoons honey (acacia honey if possible)
2 oz. ($\frac{1}{4}$ cup) lemon juice
1 tablespoon vanilla sugar
dash of Angostura bitters (optional)
hard ice cubes

Garnish: lemon slices

Method:
Shake all the ingredients together in a cocktail shaker and strain into the glasses. Garnish with lemon slices.

Parma Violet

My childhood love of candies strikes again… This
could be served either straight up in martini glasses, or
on the rocks in old-fashioned glasses. If you can find a
package of Parma violet candies, grind a few up and
sprinkle them on top.

2 martini glasses, preferably frozen, or
old-fashioned glasses

3 oz. (1^3/$_4$ jiggers) Finlandia vodka
1 oz. (^{3}/$_4$ jigger) Archer's peach schnapps
^{3}/$_4$ oz. (^{1}/$_2$ jigger) violet liqueur (Crème Yvette)
2 oz. (^{1}/$_4$ cup) lemon juice
1^1/$_2$ tablespoons sugar syrup
12 drops of orange bitters
hard ice cubes

Garnish: edible flowers

Method:
Shake all the ingredients in a cocktail shaker and fine-
strain into the glasses and garnish.

Lab and Townhouse drinks made easy

The two London bars I own have pioneered hundreds of new cocktails over the years, and—from the number of bar menus that go walkabout every week!—I suspect that customers would like to reproduce some of them at home. LAB stands for London Academy of Bartending which I founded and Townhouse is situated in a classic town-house on Beauchamp Place.

Some of the recipes are very simple—the bramble, for instance—while others call for a few exotic ingredients which you probably don't have at home. Find a recipe that everyone likes, however, and you will be surprised how quickly you can go through a bottle of limoncello or pineapple vodka.

Three Berry Daiquiri

This is a good summer alternative to other daiquiris when these fruits are in season.

2 tall goblets, sugar-rimmed

4 oz. (2$\frac{1}{2}$ jiggers) Bacardi 8-year old rum
1 oz. ($\frac{3}{4}$ jigger) Chambord (raspberry and
  blackberry liqueur)
2 oz. ($\frac{1}{4}$ cup) lemon juice
1 tablespoon sugar syrup
4 strawberries
8 raspberries
8 blackberries
crushed ice

Garnish: strawberries, raspberries, and blackberries speared on toothpicks

Method: In an electric blender, whizz all the ingredients together for 45 seconds and pour into the goblets. Garnish with the speared fruit.

Bramble

Crème de mûre is one of the best of a range of fruit liqueurs traditionally made around Dijon, in Burgundy. It has a haunting aroma of wild blackberries, and makes a very acceptable alternative to crème de cassis (black currant) in a Kir or a Kir Royale.

2 highball glasses

4 oz. (2$\frac{1}{2}$ jiggers) Plymouth or Tanquerey
  No.10 gin
2 oz. ($\frac{1}{4}$ cup) lemon juice
2 oz. ($\frac{1}{2}$ cup) sugar syrup
1 oz. ($\frac{3}{4}$ jigger) crème de mûre
crushed ice

Garnish: blackberries

Method: Half fill the highballs with crushed ice. Add the gin, lemon juice, and sugar syrup and stir both drinks. Add more crushed ice and crown with a float of crème de mûre, gently poured over the back of a spoon. Garnish with a few blackberries.

Jadoo

I was commissioned to create a cocktail list for a ritzy Indian bar and restaurant opening in Soho, London.

Seeking inspiration from the days of the Raj, I decided to base it on gin and tonic—probably the most popular drink with the colonials and their memsahibs at that time. In addition to being a great mixer for gin, quinine-flavored tonic water was effective against malaria. I also used mint, a favorite herb in India, and modestly named it Jadoo—Hindi for "magic."

2 old-fashioned glasses

12 mint leaves
1 lime, chopped
1 tablespoon superfine sugar
4 oz. (2^1/$_2$ jiggers) Bombay Sapphire gin
tonic water (to top up)
crushed ice

Garnish: sprigs of mint

Method: Muddle the mint, lime, and sugar together in the glasses, then half fill with crushed ice. Add the gin and stir. Add more ice and top up with tonic. Garnish with a sprig of mint.

Bon-bon

This cocktail takes me back to my childhood—and my unhealthy fondness for candies. With its mix of vanilla vodka, butterscotch schnapps, and limoncello, it might stretch the resources of your cocktail cabinet a little, but, for any grown-up kids, it's worth it. Usually served in martini glasses, but can also be served on the rocks in old-fashioned glasses.

2 martini glasses, preferably frozen, or old-fashioned glasses

4 oz. (2^1/$_2$ jiggers) Cariel vanilla vodka or homemade vanilla vodka (see page 29)
1 oz. (^{1}/$_2$ jigger) Teichenné butterscotch schnapps
2 oz. (1^1/$_4$ jiggers) limoncello
2 oz. (1^1/$_2$ jiggers) lemon juice
1 tablespoon vanilla sugar
hard ice cubes

Garnish: lemon fans

Method: Shake everything together in a cocktail shaker and strain into the glasses. Garnish, if you like, with lemon candies ground to a coarse powder or a lemon fan.

El Presidente Julep

I wanted a South American name for this cocktail, and a Duran Duran song inspired me to call it El Presidente.

2 large old-fashioned glasses

12 mint leaves
2 tablespoons vanilla sugar
4 oz. (2$\frac{1}{2}$ jiggers) Bacardi 8 year old rum
crushed ice

Garnish: mint leaves

Method: Bash the mint and sugar together, half in each glass, then half fill with crushed ice. Add the rum, stir, then fill to the rim with more crushed ice. Garnish with a few mint leaves.

Chelsea Rose

The perfect drink for a tipple at the Chelsea Flower Show. This cocktail overflows with the aromas and flavors of an English summer: hedgerows, orchards, and cucumber sandwiches. Hendrick's gin is actually flavored with cucumber, and also has a distinct aroma of rose petals.

2 highball glasses

4 oz. (2$\frac{1}{2}$ jiggers) Hendrick's gin
1 oz. ($\frac{1}{2}$ jigger) elderflower syrup
4 oz. ($\frac{1}{2}$ cup) cloudy apple juice, mixed with
  1 tablespoon raspberry puree (see page 29)
hard ice cubes

Garnish: apple fans and edible flowers

Method: Fill the glasses with ice cubes, then add all the ingredients and stir gently. Garnish with an apple fan and a flower.

Loretto Lemonade

Named after the town in Kentucky where Maker's Mark is distilled, a true place of pilgrimage for all bourbon aficionados.

2 highball glasses

3 oz. (1$\frac{3}{4}$ jiggers) Maker's Mark bourbon
1 oz. ($\frac{3}{4}$ jigger) Midori (melon liqueur)
1 teaspoon sugar syrup
juice of 1 lime
4 oz. ($\frac{1}{2}$ cup) cloudy apple juice
4 oz. ($\frac{1}{2}$ cup) ginger beer
hard ice cubes

Method: Half fill each glass with ice, then add the bourbon, Midori, sugar syrup, and fruit juices. Stir well, fill up with ice and top up with ginger beer.

Coleraine Cooler

Invented by one of my barmen at LAB; surprisingly enough, he is from Coleraine, Ireland. It is one cocktail I wish I had invented.

2 highball glasses

10 mint leaves
1 tablespoon vanilla sugar
2 tablespoons lime juice
4 oz. (2$\frac{1}{2}$ jiggers) Zubrowka (bison grass vodka)
1 oz. ($\frac{3}{4}$ jigger) Manzana apple liqueur
4 oz. ($\frac{1}{2}$ cup) cloudy apple juice
1 oz. ($\frac{3}{4}$ jigger) Goldschlager (cinnamon schnapps with gold leaf)
crushed ice

Garnish: apple fans dusted with cinnamon and sprigs of mint

Method: Half fill the glasses with crushed ice, add the mint, sugar, and lime juice, then stir and gently bruise the mint. Add the vodka, the Manzana, and the apple juice and stir. Add more ice and top with the Goldschlager, floated over the back of a spoon. Garnish with an apple fan and a sprig of mint.

Forbidden Fruit

This drink is a sort of high-octane Moscow Mule: Tanqueray No.10, the base spirit, is distilled with fresh botanicals rather than the usual dried juniper berries, orris root, and the rest, giving it a distinctively fresh aroma.

2 highball glasses

2 strawberries, finely chopped
4 blackberries
4 raspberries
1 tablespoon vanilla sugar
2 oz. ($1/4$ cup) lime juice
4 oz. ($2^1/2$ jiggers) Tanqueray No.10 gin
1 oz. ($1/2$ jigger) Chambord (optional)
ginger beer (to top up)
crushed ice

Garnish: slices of strawberry, blackberries, and raspberries on toothpicks and mint leaves

Method: In a cocktail shaker, muddle the fruit with the sugar, lime juice, and a little crushed ice, and pour half in each glass. Half fill the glasses with crushed ice, add the gin and Chambord (if using), and stir. Add more crushed ice, nearly to the brim, and top up with ginger beer. Garnish with the speared fruit and a few mint leaves.

Markee

My favorite bourbon cocktail, created by a friend when we first opened LAB.

2 highball or old-fashioned glasses

3 oz. ($1^3/4$ jiggers) Makers Mark bourbon
1 oz. ($^3/4$ jigger) Chambord (raspberry and
   blackberry liqueur)
2 oz. ($1/4$ cup) lemon juice
12 raspberries
4 oz. ($1/2$ cup) cranberry juice
2 teaspoons sugar syrup
hard ice cubes
crushed ice

Method: Fill both glasses with crushed ice. Shake all the ingredients together in a cocktail shaker, and fine-strain onto the crushed ice in the highball glasses.

Rapaska

An ideal drink for brunch created by my friend Jamie Terrell. As an alternative to Stolichnaya Razberi vodka, you can make your own raspberry vodka (see page 29).

2 highball glasses

3 oz. ($1^3/_4$ jiggers) Stolichnaya Razberi vodka
20 raspberries
$3^1/_2$ oz. (scant $1/_2$ cup) cloudy apple juice
$1^1/_2$ tablespoons sugar syrup
4 oz. ($1/_2$ cup) fresh orange juice
2 whole passionfruit
hard ice cubes

Garnish: 2 raspberries and sprigs of mint

Method: Shake all the ingredients in a cocktail shaker. Strain over crushed ice into the glasses and garnish with a raspberry and a sprig of mint.

Spiced Swizzle

One of the first drinks I ever created as a bartender, and very simple to make at home.

2 highball or old-fashioned glasses

$3^1/_2$ oz. ($2^1/_4$ jiggers) Sailor Jerry Spiced rum or Morgan Spiced rum
1 tablespoon sugar syrup
$1^1/_2$ oz. ($1/_2$ jigger) lime juice
$1^1/_2$ oz. ($1/_2$ jigger) amaretto Disaronno
crushed ice

Garnish: lime wheels and twists

Method: Half fill the glasses with crushed ice, add the rum, sugar syrup, and lime juice and stir. Fill up with ice, almost to the rim and top with a float of amaretto. Garnish with lime.

Jamboree

Not a drink for boy scouts, but a traditional Easter favorite for the crowd at Townhouse, who always seem to assemble for a celebratory tipple at that time of year.

2 old-fashioned glasses

$2^1/_2$ oz. ($1^3/_4$ jiggers) Wyborowa pineapple
  vodka
$1^1/_2$ oz. (1 jigger) Licor 43 (cuarenta y tres)
flesh and seeds of 4 passionfruit
1 ripe mango, peeled, pitted, and pureed
juice $^1/_2$ lemon
crushed ice
hard ice cubes

Garnish: passionfruit and mint leaves

Method: Fill the glasses with crushed ice. Shake everything else together in a cocktail shaker with the hard ice cubes, fine-strain it and pour over the crushed ice. Garnish with half a passionfruit and a few mint leaves.

Kentucky Iced Tea

Iced tea, while hugely popular in the USA and most of Europe, has never really taken off in Britain. Perhaps it just needs a helping hand...

2 highball glasses

$2^1/_2$ oz. ($1^3/_4$ jiggers) bourbon (ideally
  Buffalo Trace)
1 oz. ($^1/_2$ jigger) vanilla liqueur
3 tablespoons lemon juice
4 teaspoons vanilla sugar
12 mint leaves
iced tea (to top up), use instant, or homemade
crushed ice
hard ice cubes

Garnish: mint leaves

Method: Fill the glasses with crushed ice, then shake together all the ingredients except the tea in a cocktail shaker. Strain into the glasses and top up with tea and garnish with a few mint leaves.

Rich Dogg

The "Rich" in this cocktail is my friend Richard Hargroves, and the "Dogg"—well, I'll let you guess.

2 martini glasses, frozen and sugar-rimmed

2 teaspoons grated fresh ginger
10 green or black grapes
1 tablespoon superfine sugar
3 oz. ($1^3/_4$ jiggers) Ciroc vodka (grape-based vodka
   from France)
1 oz. ($^3/_4$ jigger) Passoa (passionfruit liqueur)
flesh and seeds of 2 passionfruit
5 teaspoons lemon juice

Garnish: 2 grapes

Method: In the glass half of a cocktail shaker, bash together the ginger, grapes, and sugar. Add the remaining ingredients, shake very hard, and fine-strain into the martini glasses. Garnish with a grape, slightly cut so you can slide it onto the rim of the glass.

Sky Cruiser

I received a bottle of peach vodka from a friend and created this cocktail, but couldn't find a name for it, so kept it in my diary. Then I flew to Japan and the plane was called Sky Cruiser—perfect.

2 martini glasses, preferably frozen

3 oz. ($1^3/_4$ jiggers) Stolichnaya peach vodka
1 oz. ($^3/_4$ jigger) Licor 43 (cuarenta y tres)
3 tablespoons lemon juice
4 teaspoons passionfruit syrup
hard ice cubes

Method: Shake all the ingredients in a cocktail shaker and fine-strain into glasses.

La Cucaracha

Sometimes, drinks just have a name that seems to suit them. La cucuracha is not an exotic Spanish dance, it's a cockroach—but it sounds good! Tequila is a difficult spirit to blend with other flavors, but this time I think I hit the spot.

Agavero is tequila-based liqueur, named after the agave cactus.

2 highball glasses

$2^1/_2$ oz. ($1^3/_4$ jiggers) Jose Cuervo
  Tequila Especial
1 oz. ($^1/_2$ jigger) Agavero
3 tablespoons lime juice
flesh and seeds of 2 passionfruit
$3^1/_2$ oz. (scant $^1/_2$ cup) cloudy apple juice
4 teaspoons vanilla sugar
crushed ice
hard ice cubes

Garnish: sprigs of mint

Method: Fill the glasses with crushed ice. Shake all the ingredients together in a cocktail shaker, strain, and pour it over the crushed ice. Garnish with a sprig of mint.

Black Bison

Zubrowka is a bison grass-flavored vodka. Bison grass only grows wild in eastern Poland, and gives the vodka a unique taste.

2 highball glasses

8 blackberries
1 tablespoon superfine sugar
4 teaspoons lemon juice
$3^1/_2$ oz. ($2^1/_4$ jiggers) Zubrowka (bison
  grass vodka)
$^3/_4$ oz. ($^1/_2$ jigger) Chambord (raspberry and
  blackberry liqueur)
$3^1/_2$ oz. (scant $^1/_2$ cup) cloudy apple juice
crushed ice

Garnish: blackberries and apple fans

Method: In a mixing glass, bash together the blackberries, sugar, and lemon juice with a scoop of crushed ice. Stir in the Zubrowka, Chambord, and apple juice, and split between the glasses. Top up with crushed ice, stir again, and garnish with a few blackberries and an apple fan.

Indian Summer

Use the rosewater you find in delicatessens, not at the cosmetics counter! Alternatively, crème de rose is a liqueur flavored with rose petals. Both are highly perfumed, so use them wisely.

2 highball glasses

10 raspberries
1 tablespoon superfine sugar
2 teaspoons rosewater (or crème de rose)
$3^1/_2$ oz. ($2^1/_4$ jiggers) Plymouth gin
4 oz. ($^1/_2$ cup) cranberry juice
crushed ice

Garnish: raspberries and sprigs of mint

Method: In a mixing glass, bash the raspberries, sugar, rosewater, and gin together with a scoop of crushed ice. Split between the 2 highball glasses, half fill with crushed ice, add the cranberry juice, stir thoroughly, and top up with more ice. Garnish with raspberries and a sprig of mint.

Madagascar Sour

A sort of autumnal variation of a lime daiquiri, made with a very good-aged rum and the delicious Xanath vanilla liqueur. Very popular at Townhouse, and named after the home of much of the world's vanilla. This is my favorite rum drink.

2 martini glasses, preferably frozen

3 oz. ($1^3/_4$ jiggers) Bacardi 8-year old rum
4 teaspoons vanilla sugar
3 tablespoons lime juice
1 oz. ($^1/_2$ jigger) Xanath vanilla liqueur

Garnish: lime wheels

Method: Shake all the ingredients together in a cocktail shaker, then fine-strain into the glasses. Garnish with a lime wheel.

Buena Vista Barfly

The classic drink greyhound uses ordinary vodka and grapefruit. This twist on the original is simple, but delicious.

2 old-fashioned glasses, sugar-rimmed

1 large pink grapefruit, peeled and cut into
   small chunks
4 teaspoons superfine sugar
$3^1/_2$ oz. ($2^1/_4$ jiggers) Wyborowa melon vodka
crushed ice

Method: In a mixing glass, muddle the fruit with the sugar, then half fill with crushed ice, add the vodka, stir, add more crushed ice and stir again. Split between the 2 glasses.

Absolutely Crushed

This was on the first menu I created for LAB. The most outrageous mix of sweet and sour and one of my favorites.

Mandarin Napoléon is a Belgian liqueur made with fresh mandarine peels from Sicily macerated with cognac and distilled three times.

2 highball glasses

4 kumquats, quartered
4 teaspoons soft brown sugar
flesh and seeds of 2 passionfruit
$3^1/_2$ oz. ($2^1/_4$ jiggers) Absolut Citron
$1^1/_2$ oz. (1 jigger) Mandarin Napoléon—if
   unavailable, use mandarine liquer
4 teaspoons lemon juice
crushed ice

Garnish: 2 kumquats

Method: In a mixing glass, muddle the kumquats, sugar, and passionfruit together with a little crushed ice. Split between the glasses and half fill them with crushed ice. Add the vodka and stir thoroughly. Fill up with crushed ice and gently crown with Mandarin Napoléon using the back of a barspoon. Garnish with kumquat halves.

Blackbird

Blackberry and apple is a wonderful autumnal combination, mixed here with the warm fragrance of vanilla.

2 highball glasses

$3^1/_2$ oz. ($2^1/_4$ jiggers) Cariel vodka or
  homemade vanilla vodka (see page 29)
8 blackberries
1 tablespoon superfine sugar
$^3/_4$ oz. (4 teaspoons) lemon juice
4 oz. ($^1/_2$ cup) cloudy apple juice
crushed ice

Garnish: blackberries and sprigs of mint

Method: In a mixing glass, bash the vodka, blackberries, sugar, and lemon juice together with a scoop of crushed ice. Divide between the glasses, half fill with crushed ice, then add the apple juice and stir thoroughly. Top up with more ice and garnish with blackberries and a sprig of mint.

Ma Cherie or Mon Cheri

A great cocktail for an indulgent occasion, like Christmas or Mother's Day. Anybody who likes liqueur chocolates will love this rich, fruity drink.

2 highball glasses

$3^1/_2$ oz. ($2^1/_4$ jiggers) Finlandia cranberry vodka
a scant oz. ($^1/_2$ jigger) Cherry Heering
  (cherry liqueur)
$1^1/_2$ oz. (1 jigger) cherry puree (see page 84)
5 teaspoons Mozart dark chocolate liqueur
5 teaspoons lemon juice
$^3/_4$ oz. ($^1/_2$ jigger) sugar syrup
$^3/_4$ oz. ($^1/_2$ jigger) club soda or 7-up (to top up)
crushed ice
hard ice cubes

Garnish: orange twists and sprigs of mint

Method: Pour the vodka, Cherry Heering, cherry puree, chocolate liqueur, lemon juice, and sugar syrup into a mixing glass, and stir well with hard ice cubes.

Half fill each glass with crushed ice, split the drink between the 2, stir, fill up with crushed ice, and top up with soda or 7-Up. Stir again gently to mix all the ingredients and garnish with orange twists and a sprig of mint.

Monarch

A drink conceived in 2002 while I was coming up with new drinks for Townhouse. This creation was inspired by the Queen's Golden Jubilee that year; as I walked through Green Park the week before I thought about what was quintessentially English. Featuring her late mother's favorite tipple, gin, this is my favorite gin drink and I'm very proud of it. It's best to give the glasses 1 hour in the freezer first.

2 martini glasses, preferably frozen

$3\frac{1}{2}$ oz. ($2\frac{1}{4}$ jiggers) Plymouth gin
1 oz. ($\frac{1}{2}$ jigger) elderflower syrup
$1\frac{1}{2}$ oz. (1 jigger) lemon juice
4 teaspoons sugar syrup
8–10 drops peach bitters (optional)
8 mint leaves
hard ice cubes

Garnish: lemon twists (optional)

Method: Shake all the ingredients in a cocktail shaker, fine-strain into the glasses and garnish with a twist of lemon, if you like.

Rumba

I made this drink with a bizarre vanilla liqueur but didn't think it was perfect, until Xanath came onto the market, which totally changed the flavor and made the drink amazing.

2 old-fashioned glasses

3 oz. ($1\frac{3}{4}$ jiggers) Appleton VX rum
$\frac{3}{4}$ oz. ($\frac{1}{2}$ jigger) Xanath vanilla liqueur
2 tablespoons Greek yogurt
$3\frac{1}{2}$ oz. (scant $\frac{1}{2}$ cup) cloudy apple juice
1 tablespoon vanilla sugar
hard ice cubes

Garnish: apple fans dusted with cinnamon

Method: Fill both glasses with ice, then shake all the ingredients together in a cocktail shaker and split between the glasses. Garnish with an apple fan.

Kool Hand Luke

My friend Jamie Terrell invented this drink so I have named it after his son Luke. Paul Newman would probably drink it with hard-boiled eggs.

2 highball glasses

2 fresh limes, quartered
4 teaspoons soft brown sugar
8 drops Angostura bitters
$3^1/_2$ oz. ($2^1/_4$ jiggers) Myers's rum
crushed ice

Method: In a mixing glass, muddle the limes, sugar, and Angostura bitters together with a little crushed ice. Divide between the glasses and half fill each with crushed ice. Add the rum, stir, then fill up with more crushed ice and stir again.

Ruby Tuesday

Probably the most difficult drink to make in the world! Much easier to play on the guitar. There are just so many ingredients and the balance must be just right, but the finished product is incredible. This is the drink to have at Townhouse.

If you can't find cherry puree, stone 25 ripe cherries and blend them with a little sugar syrup, or use 3 tablespoons blended canned cherries.

2 martini glasses, preferably frozen or old-fashioned glasses

3 oz. (2 jiggers) Finlandia Cranberry vodka
$^3/_4$ oz. ($^1/_2$ jigger) Midori (melon liqueur)
$^3/_4$ oz. ($^1/_2$ jigger) Mandarin Napoléon
  (orange liqueur)
$^3/_4$ oz. ($^1/_2$ jigger) Licor 43 (cuarenta y tres)
4 teaspoons lemon juice
2 tablespoons cranberry juice
flesh and seeds of 2 passionfruit
$1^1/_2$ oz. (1 jigger) cherry puree
4 teaspoons passionfruit syrup
4 x $^3/_4$-inch cubes of watermelon
hard ice cubes
crushed ice (if serving in old-fashioned
  glasses)

Method: Shake all the ingredients in a cocktail shaker, or preferably a tin shaker (to ensure all the ingredients fit). Shake until well mixed and strain into the glasses.

Queen of Bahia

This drink is named for a very attractive Brazilian waitress!

2 old-fashioned glasses

2 fresh limes, chopped in 12 half wedges
4 fresh strawberries
2 tablespoons dark soft brown sugar
$3\frac{1}{2}$ oz. ($2\frac{1}{4}$ jiggers) cachaça (sugar cane spirit)
1 oz. ($\frac{1}{2}$ jigger) crème de fraise
crushed ice

Garnish: strawberry fans dusted with icing sugar

Method: In a mixing glass, muddle the limes and strawberries together with the sugar, and split between the glasses. Add cachaça to both, half fill with crushed ice, stir and fill up with ice. Crown with a dribble of crème de fraise. Garnish with a strawberry fan.

Bisonite

Zubrowka and apple juice is a Polish classic: this is a refined version.

2 martini glasses

$3\frac{1}{2}$ oz. ($2\frac{1}{4}$ jiggers) Zubrowka (bison grass vodka)
3 tablespoons cloudy apple juice
1 oz. (2 tablespoons) passionfruit syrup
2 drops of peach bitters (optional)
2 teaspoons lemon juice
hard ice cubes

Garnish: apple fans

Method: Shake all the ingredients in a cocktail shaker, then fine-strain into the glasses. Garnish with an apple fan.

Metropolis

I created this for the Absolut Mandrin launch in London.

2 old-fashioned glasses

2$\frac{1}{2}$ oz. (1$\frac{3}{4}$ jiggers) Absolut Mandrin
1 oz. ($\frac{1}{2}$ jigger) Mandarin Napoléon
  (orange liqueur)
3 tablespoons lemon juice
4 teaspoons sugar syrup
hard ice cubes

Garnish: orange twists

Method: Fill both glasses with ice cubes, then shake all the ingredients in a cocktail shaker, strain, and divide between the glasses. Garnish with twists of orange.

Very Berry

This is a bestseller at LAB.

2 old-fashioned glasses

1 fresh lime, cut into 12 half wedges
12 blackberries
2 tablespoons superfine sugar
3$\frac{1}{2}$ oz. (2$\frac{1}{4}$ jiggers) vodka
1 oz. ($\frac{1}{2}$ jigger) crème de mûre
crushed ice

Method: Put the lime in a mixing glass with the blackberries, sugar, and vodka and muddle all the ingredients together. Split between the 2 glasses, add half the crushed ice and stir. Top up each glass with crushed ice. Gently crown the finished cocktails with the crème de mûre, and serve.

Vitamina

A perfect revitalising drink for a Sunday afternoon. An alternative to a Virgin or Bloody Mary—if you want vodka add about 3 oz. for the 2 glasses.

2 highball glasses

5 oz. ($^2/_3$ cup) fresh carrot juice
2 teaspoons celery salt
2 teaspoons Worcestershire sauce
2 teaspoons lemon juice
6 drops Tabasco
hard ice cubes

Garnish: carrot and cherry tomatoes

Method: In a mixing glass, stir everything together with hard ice cubes. Pour into the glasses and garnish with long shavings of carrot and cherry tomatoes.

Honey Caipirinha

Perfect for the cocktail fan who wants to avoid refined sugar: in fact, any caipirinha or caipiroska recipe works very well with honey instead of sugar syrup or sugar.

2 old-fashioned glasses

1 lime, cut into 12 half wedges
3 tablespoons runny honey
$3^1/_2$ oz. ($2^1/_4$ jiggers) cachaça (sugar
  cane spirit)
crushed ice

Method: Muddle the lime and honey together in a mixing glass, then add a scoop of crushed ice and the cachaça. Stir thoroughly and divide between the glasses. Add more crushed ice to top up and then stir again.

Mango Caipirinha

An exotic twist on a classic.

2 old-fashioned glasses

1 lime, cut into 12 half wedges
3–4 slices ripe mango
1 tablespoon superfine sugar
$3\frac{1}{2}$ oz. ($2\frac{1}{4}$ jiggers) cachaça (sugar
 cane spirit)
crushed ice

Garnish: mango fans

Method: Muddle the lime, mango, and sugar
together in a mixing glass, then add a scoop
of crushed ice and the cachaça. Stir
thoroughly and divide between the glasses,
adding more crushed ice to top up and then
stir again. Garnish with a mango fan.

Champagne Cocktail

This is my favorite champagne cocktail.

Licor 43 (cuarenta y tres) is a bright yellow Spanish liqueur made from citrus and fruit juices, flavored with vanilla and other aromatic herbs and spices, apparently, with 43 different ingredients in total.

2 champagne flutes

1 small orange, peeled and carefully cut into
  skinless segments
$\frac{1}{2}$ oz. ($\frac{1}{3}$ jigger) Licor 43 (cuarenta y tres)
4 drops orange bitters
2 white sugar cubes
1 oz. ($\frac{3}{4}$ jigger) Woodford Reserve bourbon
champagne (to top up)

Method: Marinate the orange segments in the Licor 43 for an hour or so. Drip 2 drops of bitters on each sugar cube, put 1 in each glass, and carefully split the bourbon between the glasses.

Almost fill the glasses with champagne and drop a marinated orange segment into each glass.

Classic and Neo-Classic Cocktails

Many classic cocktails date from the turn of the 20th Century, when ingredients were very limited. Gin, rum, whisky, or brandy would simply be mixed with whatever was available to the bartender: often just sugar, ice, and lemon juice.

As communications improved and the world grew smaller, cocktails became much more inventive. Ideas and ingredients spread around the globe: nowadays, new and exciting drinks are within everybody's grasp, and even the average supermarket will stock everything you need to make great drinks at home.

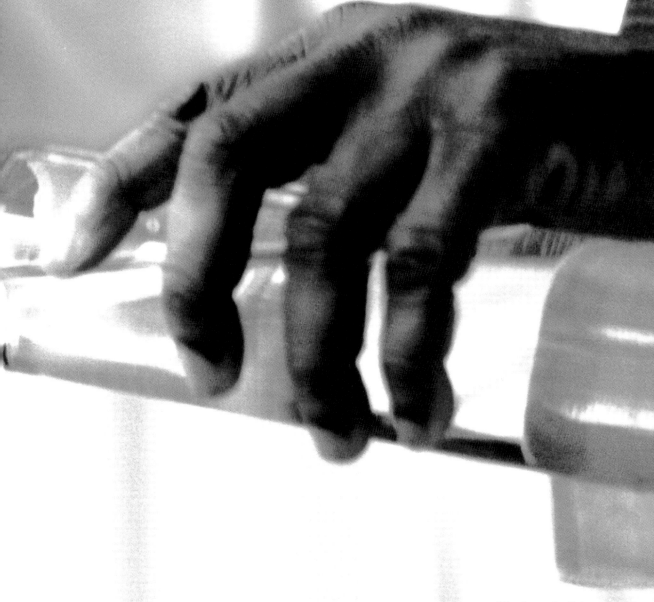

Bloody Mary

This drink was created at Harry's New York Bar in Paris in the early 1920s. This is the quintessential vodka cocktail and my favorite vodka classic. The point of a Bloody Mary is to invigorate, not to send you back to bed, so it should never be mind-numbingly strong. Nor does it need dozens of ingredients: Worcestershire sauce and lemon juice are all the tomato and vodka really need.

2 highball glasses

$2^1/_2$ oz. ($1^3/_4$ jiggers) vodka, Ciroc (grape-based vodka from France) for preference
2 tablespoons Worcestershire sauce
2 teaspoons Tabasco (optional)
1 teaspoon celery salt
juice $^1/_2$ lemon
8oz. (1 cup) tomato juice
hard ice cubes

Garnish: celery sticks and cherry tomatoes.

Method: Fill each glass with ice, then add the rest of the ingredients, stirring all the time. Garnish with a celery stick and a couple of cherry tomatoes.

Japanese Slipper

This classic uses Midori, the curious and distinctive bright green melon liqueur from Japan.

2 martini glasses, preferably frozen

$1^1/_2$ oz. (1 jigger) Midori
3oz. (2 jiggers) Jose Cuervo Especial tequila
3 tablespoons lime juice
2 oz. ($^1/_4$ cup) fresh pineapple juice
hard ice cubes

Method: Shake all the ingredients in a cocktail shaker and strain into the glasses.

Caipiroska

The vodka-based version of a caipirinha.

2 old-fashioned glasses

2 limes, each cut in 12 half wedges
2 tablespoons superfine sugar
$3^1/_2$ oz. ($2^1/_4$ jiggers) vodka
crushed ice

Method: In a mixing glass, muddle the limes together with the sugar, then split them between the glasses. Half fill each glass with crushed ice, add the vodka, stir, top up with ice and stir again.

Caipirinha

A favorite peasant drink in Brazil, where cachaça—a sugar cane spirit—is cheap and mostly, to be frank, rather crudely made. However, the new popularity of caipirinhas has led to some much better cachaças being distilled.

2 old-fashioned glasses

2 limes, each cut in 12 half wedges
2 tablespoons superfine sugar (or soft
  brown sugar)
$3^1/_2$ oz. ($2^1/_4$ jiggers) cachaça
crushed ice

Method:In a mixing glass muddle the limes together with the sugar, then split between the glasses. Half fill each glass with crushed ice, add the cachaça, stir, top up with ice and stir again.

Caipirinha for 6 people

6 old-fashioned glasses

14 oz. ($1^3/_4$ cups) cachaça
4 oz. ($^1/_2$ cup) sugar syrup
5 oz. ($^2/_3$ cup) freshly squeezed lime juice
2 tablespoons superfine sugar
hard ice cubes

Method: Fill up a $1^3/_4$-quart pitcher with hard cubed ice. Stir all the ingredients in the pitcher with a ladle, then serve over fresh, hard ice cubes in the old-fashioned glasses.

Margarita

This classic tequila cocktail, named after a famous Texan socialite, is best made with a young, unwooded tequila. Freshly squeezed lime juice is essential.

2 martini or old-fashioned glasses, rimmed (or only half-rimmed) with lime juice and salt

2½ oz. (1¾ jiggers) tequila
1oz. (½ jigger) Cointreau
3 tablespoons lime juice
hard ice cubes
crushed ice (if serving in old-fashioned glasses)

Garnish: lime wheels

Method: Shake all the ingredients in a cocktail shaker and strain into the glasses and garnish with a wheel of lime.

Manhattan

A classic cocktail which can be served in three different ways—sweet, perfect, or dry—depending upon whether Italian sweet vermouth, French dry vermouth, or a mixture of the two is used.

The method is the same for all three: put all ingredients into a cocktail shaker, shake with hard ice cubes, strain into glasses, and garnish. Serve in martini glasses, preferably frozen, although all three can be served on the rocks in old-fashioned glasses if preferred.

Manhattan Sweet

3½ oz. (2¼ jiggers) rye whiskey
¾ oz. (½ jigger) red vermouth
2 drops of Angostura bitters

Garnish: maraschino cherries

Manhattan Perfect

3½ oz. (2¼ jiggers) rye whiskey
2 teaspoons (¼ jigger) red vermouth
2 teaspoons (¼ jigger) dry vermouth
2 drops Angostura bitters

Garnish: orange twists

Manhattan Dry

3½ oz. (2¼ jiggers) rye whiskey
¾ oz. (½ jigger) dry vermouth
2 drops Angostura bitters

Garnish: lemon twists

Millionaire

A classic cocktail which merits a revival. It can be served straight up in a martini glass or on the rocks in an old-fashioned glass.

2 martini glasses, preferably frozen and sugar-rimmed, or old-fashioned glasses

2½ oz. (1¾ jiggers) Jack Daniels
1 teaspoon grenadine
1 teaspoon sugar syrup
3 tablspoons lemon juice
hard ice cubes

Garnish: lemon wheels

Method: Shake everything together in a cocktail shaker, then fine-strain into the glasses. Garnish with a lemon wheel.

Champagne Cocktail

The perfect way to start a celebration—Christmas morning springs to mind. Just don't have more than two!

2 champagne flutes

6 drops Angostura bitters
2 white sugar cubes
1oz. (¾ jiggers) cognac
champagne (to top up)

Method: Drip 3 drops of bitters onto each sugar cube, put 1 in each glass, split the cognac between each glass, and top up with champagne. Don't stir!

Mint Julep

The classic all-American cocktail. The sort of drink to sip on a humid afternoon on a verandah in the deep South, as the ceiling fan turns slowly and the cicadas chirrup.

2 old-fashioned glasses

16 mint leaves
2 tablespoons superfine sugar
$3^1/_2$ oz. ($2^1/_4$ jiggers) bourbon
crushed ice

Garnish: sprigs of mint

Method: In a mixing glass, muddle the mint leaves and sugar together with a little of the bourbon and some crushed ice, and split between the glasses. Half fill each glass with crushed ice, add the rest of the bourbon, stir, and top up with crushed ice. Garnish with a sprig of mint.

Rusty Nail

Drambuie's mix of Scotch, herbs, and honey makes a particularly warming liqueur. This famous old cocktail is best served after a good dinner on a cold night. This is a great Father's Day drink.

2 old-fashioned glasses

$3^1/_2$ oz. ($2^1/_4$ jiggers) Scotch whisky
$1^1/_2$ oz. (1 jigger) Drambuie
hard ice cubes

Method: Fill each glass with ice, then split the Scotch and Drambuie between them and stir until well mixed.

Screwdriver

This famous (and famously simple) cocktail relies entirely on the quality of the ingredients, especially the orange juice, which if possible should be squeezed just before using, and fine-strained to remove any bits of pulp. This is a cocktail that benefits from being well mixed, which some bars just don't do. Legend has it that the name derives from a Texan oil man who stirred his drink with a screwdriver.

2 highball glasses

4 oz. ($2\frac{1}{2}$ jiggers) Ketel One vodka
8 oz. (1 cup) freshly squeezed orange juice
hard ice cubes

Garnish: orange slices

Method: Fill each glass with ice, split the vodka between them and top up with fresh orange. Stir extremely well and garnish with an orange slice.

Mojito

Cuba's national drink, served everywhere in Havana and now popular all over the world. Very addictive, and not as acidic as margaritas and caipirinhas.

2 old-fashioned glasses

1 fresh lime, cut into 12 half wedges
14 mint leaves
4 teaspoons superfine sugar
$3\frac{1}{2}$ oz. ($2\frac{1}{4}$ jiggers) Havana Club 3 year-old rum or Bacardi 8-year old rum
club soda (to top up)
crushed ice

Garnish: sprigs of mint

Method: In a mixing glass, muddle together the lime with the mint, sugar and a little crushed ice, and split between the glasses. Half fill each glass with crushed ice, stir, add the rum, stir again, then top up with crushed ice and soda. Garnish with a sprig of mint.

Mojito for 6 people

6 old-fashioned glasses

12 oz. ($1\frac{1}{2}$ cups) Havana Club 3 year-old rum or Barcadi 8-year old rum
5 oz. ($\frac{2}{3}$ cup) freshly squeezed lime juice
4 oz. ($\frac{1}{2}$ cup) sugar syrup
2 tablespoons superfine sugar
4 oz. ($\frac{1}{2}$ cup) club soda
20 mint leaves
2 whole limes, quartered
hard ice cubes

Method: Fill up a $1\frac{1}{2}$-quart pitcher with hard ice cubes. Add all the ingredients and then stir with a ladle until well mixed. Pour into the glasses with fresh hard ice cubes.

Moscow Mule

2 highball glasses

juice of 1 lime
4 oz. (2½ jiggers) vodka
ginger beer (to top up)
hard ice cubes

Garnish: ginger slices and
sprigs of mint

Method: Half fill each glass
with ice cubes, add the lime
juice and vodka, stir, then fill
up each glass with ice and
top up with ginger beer.
Garnish with thinly sliced
ginger and a sprig of mint.

This cocktail was created in America when
Russian vodka began to be imported. The
quality of the ginger beer is vital here: for a
proper mule-kick, use a powerful variety: Idris
Hot is good, or, even better, Fentiman's
naturally brewed ginger beer, if you can find it.

Negroni

Invented in Florence, but popular everywhere, and a great standby in pubs and airport lounges, where all three components of the Negroni can usually be found. Punt e Mes is often used in place of red vermouth: you might also try Vya, from California, or the hard-to-find Noilly Prat red. It can also be served with club soda in a highball.

2 old-fashioned glasses

2 oz. (1¼ jiggers) Plymouth gin
1 oz. (1½ jiggers) red vermouth
1 oz. (1½ jiggers) Campari
hard ice cubes

Garnish: orange slices

Method: Fill each glass with ice cubes, stir all the ingredients together in a mixing glass, then pour over the rocks in the glasses and garnish with orange slices.

Old Fashioned

A bartender's favorite—as long as the bar's not too busy—this is the one recipe in which making two drinks at once doesn't really work, so the ingredients below are for one.

1 old-fashioned glass (naturally enough)

1 brown sugar cube
1 dash orange bitters
1 dash Angostura bitters
1 teaspoon club soda
1½ oz (1 jigger) .Woodford Reserve bourbon
hard ice cubes

Garnish: strip of orange zest

Method: A good old fashioned takes several minutes to make, and involves muddling the sugar, bitters, and club soda together while adding bourbon and ice cubes: the sugar needs to be more or less dissolved before you can start adding ice. Do it patiently, and the drink will be clear and well balanced, with the orange zest adding the vital fragrance.

Sidecar

Perhaps sensibly named for a motorcycle's passenger, not the driver.

2 martini glasses, preferably frozen

1½ oz. (1 jigger) Cognac or Remy Grand Cru
1½ oz. (1 jigger) Cointreau
3 tablespoons fresh lemon juice
1 teaspoon superfine sugar
hard ice cubes

Method: Shake all the ingredients in a cocktail shaker, then fine-strain into the glasses.

Tequila Sunrise

The most instantly recognizable cocktail in the world, with dark red grenadine gently drifting into orange juice.

2 highball glasses

4 oz. (2½ jiggers) Jose Cuervo Especial tequila
8 oz. (1 cup) freshly squeesed orange juice
2 teaspoons grenadine
hard ice cubes

Garnish: orange slices and fresh cherries

Method: Fill both glasses with ice, pour in the tequila, add the orange juice and carefully float the grenadine on top.

Silk Stocking

Or, in fact, a pair of stockings.

This was very popular in the 80s. I have reinvented it with a scoop of ice cream—it can be any flavor, but preferably raspberry.

2 martini glasses

3 oz. (2 jiggers) Jose Cuervo Especial tequila
4 teaspoons grenadine
1½ oz (1 jigger) white crème de cacao
3 tablespoons light cream
2 teaspoons superfine sugar
1 scoop soft raspberry ice cream
crushed ice

Garnish: raspberries and cinnamon dust

Method: Whizz all the ingredients in a blender for 30 seconds or so, pour into the glasses and garnish with the raspberries and cinnamon dust.

White Russian

The two Russians, white and black, have been popular after-dinner cocktails for decades, especially before Bailey's and a host of similar cream liqueurs arrived. Both drinks can be served with a small scoop of ice cream on top: vanilla in the White Russian and chocolate or coffee in the Black Russian. You could even have them for dessert. You should use Russian vodka for these, naturally.

2 old-fashioned glasses

1$^1/_2$ oz (1 jigger) vodka
1$^1/_2$ oz (1 jigger) Kahlua
4 oz. ($^1/_2$ cup) light cream
2 scoops soft vanilla ice cream
hard ice cubes

Method: Fill both glasses with ice, pour half the vodka in each, then add the Kahlua and cream and stir. Place the ice cream on top.

Black Russian

2 old-fashioned glasses

3 oz. (2 jiggers) vodka
1$^1/_2$ oz (1 jigger) Kahlua
2 scoops soft chocolate
  or coffee ice cream
hard ice cubes

Method: Fill both glasses with ice, pour half the vodka in each, then add the Kahlua and stir. Place the ice cream on top.

West Indian Rum Colada

Based on the classic Pina Colada, but updated to get away from the drink's slightly dubious reputation. Tropical and deeply refreshing.

2 large wine glasses

4 oz. (2$\frac{1}{2}$ jiggers) Bacardi Oro
$\frac{1}{3}$ cup fresh pineapple chunks
3 tablespoons coconut cream (Coco Lopez)
3 tablespoons light cream
4 drops Angostura bitters
2 pinches of salt
crushed ice

Method: Fill both glasses with crushed ice. Whizz all the ingredients together in a blender, along with a scoop of crushed ice and pour into the glasses.

Whisk(e)y Sour

Sours can be made with any dark spirit, and are the simplest versions of the strong, sweet, sour, weak cocktail equation. You can drink it straight up in a martini glass or on the rocks in an old-fashioned. My favorite whisky cocktail; use whichever brand you like best.

2 martini glasses, preferably frozen, or old-fashioned glasses

4 oz. (2$\frac{1}{2}$ jiggers) Scotch/Rye/Irish/
  Bourbon/Canadian
3 tablespoons lemon juice
4 teaspoons supefine sugar
4 dashes Angostura bitters
hard ice cubes

Garnish: cherries and lemon twists

Method: Shake all the ingredients in a cocktail shaker and strain into the glasses. Serve with a cherry and a lemon twist.

Famous drinks in bars and hotels

Cocktails taste even better if you drink them in the right place. These bars and hotels are synonymous with one particular drink. In most cases, the drink was created there; in the case of Duke's Hotel, it is simply the best place in the world to enjoy a martini.

Duke's Hotel, London

Perhaps the most famous cocktail of them all, with countless variations and plenty of attached myths and legends. Nobody can be sure who created it, but it is often credited to an Italian bartender working in New York during the early part of the 20th Century.

In London, the best martini is at Duke's Hotel, in St James's. The bar manager serves 100 a day, all from a special trolley wheeled into the traditionally decorated bar.

The first documented dry martini recipe specified Plymouth Gin. It appeared in Stuart's *Fancy Drinks and How to Mix Them* in 1896.

A martini has a lifespan of about 5 minutes. It needs to be ice cold to be enjoyed properly.

The Classic Martini

Glass	2 martini glasses, preferably frozen
Ingredients	4 dashes of dry French vermouth
	5 oz. (3¼ jiggers) Plymouth Gin
	frozen hard ice cubes (if the gin isn't frozen)
Garnish	2 pitted olives or twists of lemon
Method	Pour half the vermouth into each glass, turn them carefully so each glass is coated, then pour out any residue. If you are using frozen gin, simply pour it into the glasses; if it's not frozen, stir the gin with the ice in a mixing glass and strain into the glasses. Garnish with the olives or lemon and drink before it warms up.

The Singapore Sling

Glass	2 highball glasses
Ingredients	3 oz. (1³/₄ jiggers) Bombay Sapphire gin
	3 tablespoons lemon juice
	generous dash of sugar syrup
	4 oz. (¹/₂ cup) ginger ale
	1 oz. (¹/₂ jigger) Cherry Heering (float)
	1 oz. (¹/₂ jigger) Bénédictine (float)
	hard ice cubes
Garnish	lemon fans
Method	Fill both glasses with ice cubes. In a mixing glass, stir together the gin, lemon juice, and sugar syrup, then split between the glasses. Top up with ginger ale, and carefully float the 2 liqueurs on top. Garnish with a lemon fan.

Harry's Bar, Venice

This cocktail was created by Giuseppe Cipriani at Harry's Bar in Venice in 1948, and named after a painter, Giovan Battista Bellini, who had an exhibition of his work in Venice at the time. Harry's Bar also invented the dish carpaccio of beef, named after the Renaissance artist Vittore Carpaccio.

Should you ever visit Harry's Bar, sit at the bar: it's cheaper, the bar snacks are free, and you can admire the skill and longevity of the barmen as they top up dozens of glasses of white peach puree with prosecco. Use a good, fizzy (spumante) prosecco: Bisol is an excellent brand.

The Bellini

Glass	2 champagne flutes
Ingredients	2 fresh peaches, pitted and chopped (white peaches if possible)
	1 oz. (½ jigger) crème de pêche
	prosecco or champagne (to top)
Method	Blend the peaches with the crème de pêche. Strain and divide between the glasses. Top up with prosecco or champagne, stir gently, and serve.

El Floridita, Havana

Invented by an American engineer called Jennings Cox, while working in a mining town called Daiquiri, in Cuba. He normally drank gin, but his supply had run out and so he devised a cocktail based on the local rum.

El Floridita and the nearby Bodeguita del Medio are Havana's two most famous bars, partly because that ubiquitous drinker Ernest Hemingway frequented both establishments. Scrawled on the wall in Bodeguita is the legend, "My mojito in Bodeguita, my daiquiri in Floridita": perhaps not the finest poetry Papa H. ever wrote, but a useful *aide memoire* for the alcoholically challenged.

The Daiquiri

Glass	2 martini glasses
Ingredients	4 oz. (2$^{1}/_{2}$ jiggers) Havana Club rum
	3 tablespoons lime juice
	4 teaspoons superfine sugar
	hard ice cubes
Garnish	wheels of lime
Method	Shake all the ingredients together in a cocktail shaker, then fine-strain into the glasses. Garnish with a lime wheel.

Trader Vics, Oakland

Originally made with a fine, golden, medium-bodied Jamaican rum from Kingston, with inspiration from a Havana barman. Returning to Oakland after a trip to Cuba, Trader Vic added fresh lime juice, flavored and sweetened it with orange curacao and almond-flavored orgeat syrup. The mai tai became hugely popular in his Oakland bar, and can now be enjoyed in Trader Vics bars all over the world.

This version is based on the original 1944 recipe.

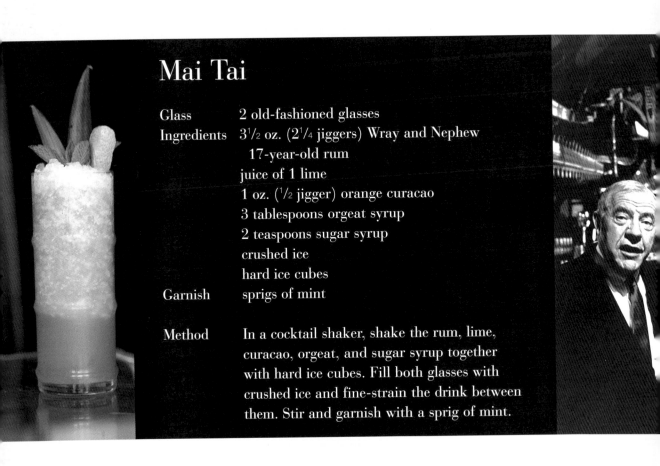

Mai Tai

Glass	2 old-fashioned glasses
Ingredients	3½ oz. (2¼ jiggers) Wray and Nephew 17-year-old rum
	juice of 1 lime
	1 oz. (½ jigger) orange curacao
	3 tablespoons orgeat syrup
	2 teaspoons sugar syrup
	crushed ice
	hard ice cubes
Garnish	sprigs of mint
Method	In a cocktail shaker, shake the rum, lime, curacao, orgeat, and sugar syrup together with hard ice cubes. Fill both glasses with crushed ice and fine-strain the drink between them. Stir and garnish with a sprig of mint.

Moneypenny

2 highball glasses

20 fresh raspberries
flesh and seeds of 2 passionfruit
4 teaspoons sugar syrup
4 oz. ($\frac{1}{2}$ cup) cloudy apple juice
4 oz. ($\frac{1}{2}$ cup) orange juice
crushed ice

Garnish: apple fans, raspberries, and sprigs of mint

Method: Gently muddle the raspberries, passionfruit, and sugar syrup together with some crushed ice in a mixing glass and split between the glasses. Add more crushed ice and the fruit juices, stir, fill up with ice and garnish with an apple fan, raspberries, and a sprig of mint.

Holly Goodhead

2 highball glasses

20 fresh raspberries
4 oz. (¹/₂ cup) cranberry juice
2 tablespoons vanilla sugar
2 tablespoons plain yogurt
crushed ice

Method: Fill both glasses with crushed ice,
blend the other ingredients together and split
between the glasses.

May Day

2 highball glasses

2 ripe peaches, pitted and roughly chopped
4 strawberries, cubed
flesh and seeds of 2 passionfruit
4 oz. (¹/₂ cup) cloudy apple juice
1 tablespoons superfine sugar
2 teaspoons grated fresh ginger
crushed ice

Garnish: apple fans

Method: Blend all the ingredients together
with crushed ice and split between the
glasses. Garnish with an apple fan.

There's nothing wrong with giving children the taste for cocktails: without alcohol, naturally… and "naturally" is the right word to describe this delicious, healthy, vitamin-packed drink: just don't let the grown-ups drink it all. Mind you, it's very good with a splash of dark rum, which makes it a Honey Rydes Again…

Honey Ryder

2 highball glasses or large goblets

4 oz. ($1/2$ cup) fresh orange juice
flesh and seeds of 2 passionfruit
1 banana, skinned and roughly chopped
2 tablespoons plain yogurt
4 teaspoons honey (acacia for preference)
4 teaspoons raw sugar
crushed ice

To garnish: 6 slices of fresh ripe banana and
grated nutmeg

Method: Whizz everything together in a
blender with a scoop of crushed ice. Fill the
glasses with crushed ice and pour in the
drink.

Cut the 3 slices of banana from edge to
center, dust them with grated nutmeg and
carefully slide them over the rim of the glass.
Drink with a straw.

Christmas Jones

A fizzy drink for the nuclear expert in *The
World is Not Enough*.

2 highball glasses

4 fresh strawberries
2 teaspoons superfine sugar
5 oz ($2/3$ cup) pineapple juice
7-Up (to top)
hard ice cubes

Garnish: slices of strawberry and sprigs of mint

Method: In a blender, whizz the strawberries,
sugar, and pineapple juice together. Fill both
glasses with ice, split the mixture between the
glasses and top up with 7-Up. Garnish with
slices of strawberry and a sprig of mint.

Jinx

Halle Berry is my favorite Bond girl and this drink matches the color of her bikini in *Die Another Day*.

2 highball glasses

1 ripe mango, pitted,
  skinned and chopped roughly
8 fresh raspberries
4 oz. (1/2 cup) cloudy apple juice
4 teaspoons vanilla sugar
2 tablespoons plain yogurt
crushed ice

Garnish: slices of mango and sprigs of mint

Method: Fill both glasses with crushed ice, then blend all the ingredients together in a blender, along with a scoop of crushed ice and then pour into the glasses. Garnish with a slice of mango and a sprig of mint.

Kissy Suzuki

To make your own raspberry puree see page 29.

2 highball glasses

3 tablespoons raspberry puree
3 tablespoons cranberry juice
5 oz. (2/3 cup) cloudy apple juice
7-Up (to top up)
crushed or cubed ice

Garnish: strawberries

Method: Half fill both glasses with ice cubes. In a cocktail shaker, shake together the raspberry puree, cranberry juice, and apple juice with ice cubes. Split between the glasses, top up with 7-Up, and garnish with strawberries.

Lupe Lamora

2 highball glasses

1 ripe fresh pear, cored and cut into chunks
20 fresh raspberries
flesh and seeds of 2 passionfruit
4 oz. ($^1/_2$ cup) cloudy apple juice
4 teaspoons raw sugar
crushed ice

Garnish: raspberries and sprigs of mint

Method: Fill both glasses with ice, then blend the fruit, juices, and sugar together in a blender, along with a scoop of crushed ice and split between the glasses – you can fine-strain the drink to get rid of the seeds if you like. Garnish with raspberries and sprigs of mint.

Pussy Galore

A golden drink for the unforgettable bond girl in *Goldfinger*.

2 highball glasses

2 oz. ($^1/_4$ cup) orange juice
2 oz. ($^1/_4$ cup) cloudy apple juice
1 fresh mango, skinned and chopped
1 tablespoon vanilla sugar
2 teaspoons grated fresh ginger
crushed ice

Garnish: apple fans

Method: Whizz everything together in a blender, along with crushed ice and split between the glasses. Garnish with an apple fan.

A brightly colored drink to go with her vibrant hair in *Diamonds are Forever*.

2 highball glasses

1 fresh ripe banana, peeled and
  roughly chopped
1 fresh ripe mango, pitted, peeled, and
  roughly chopped
flesh and seeds of 2 passionfruit
8 fresh raspberries
4 oz. (1/2 cup) cloudy apple juice
4 teaspoons vanilla sugar
2 tablespoons plain low-fat yogurt
crushed ice

Garnish: slices of mango and sprigs of mint.

Method: Blend all the ingredients together in a blender along with a scoop of crushed ice and split between the glasses, straining if you want to. Garnish with slices of mango and a sprig of mint.

It's definitely worth investing in a bottle of real maple syrup for this drink: the cheaper flavored corn syrups are tasteless by comparison.

2 highball glasses

4 teaspoons grrenadine, plus extra to rim the
  glasses
superfine sugar for coating rim
1 tablespoon chocolate sauce for coating
  inside glass
14 oz. (1³/₄ cups) milk
4 teaspoons maple syrup
crushed ice
hard ice cubes

Method: First, dampen the rim of each glass with a little grenadine, and coat with superfine sugar. Then carefully squirt chocolate sauce around the inside of each glass.

Fill each glass with crushed ice. In a cocktail shaker, shake together the milk, grenadine, and maple syrup with hard ice cubes. Strain and split between the glasses.

Entertaining
at home

These recipes are for 6, 12, 18, and 24, but
you can adapt them to however many people
you have at your party, just keep the
proportions the same.
To complement your stylish cocktails, we
have given you a few ideas for canapés,
created by my good friend Robert Reed.

Cosmopolitan Punch

The success of *Sex and the City* has given this classic a new lease of life.

This is the perfect party drink: it's easy to make in a big punchbowl, and it actually benefits from being made the night before, so that the fruit can marinate in the alcohol. Remember to stick a few martini glasses in the freezer; otherwise, you could serve it on the rocks in old-fashioned glasses.

Serves 6

Glasses: 6 martini glasses, preferably frozen

Ingredients: 2 whole oranges, cut up
6 whole limes, cut up
flesh and seeds of 4 passionfruit
6 strawberries, quartered
6 raspberries
7 oz. (scant cup) Absolut Citron vodka
3 oz. (2 jiggers) Cointreau
2 oz. ($^{1}/_{4}$ cup) fresh lime juice
5 oz. ($^{2}/_{3}$ cup) cranberry juice

Method: Put all the fruit into a punchbowl, pour in the vodka, Cointreau, and juices, and give it a gentle stir. Cover the bowl with plastic wrap and put it in the fridge. When you're ready to serve it, give it another gentle stir and ladle it into glasses.

Bourbon Street Punch

When I worked at Smollensky's I used to make a *Bourbon Street breeze*. I liked the name but wanted to make it into a punch and so added the warming flavors of vanilla, apples, and raisins.

To infuse bourbon with raisins, simply push about 12 good-quality, large raisins into the bottle and leave for 1–2 weeks, shaking occasionally.

This drink can be prepared several hours in advance.

Serves 12

Glass: 12 old-fashioned glasses
Ingredients: 14 oz. (1³/₄ cups) raisin-infused
        Woodford Reserve bourbon
    8 oz. (1 cup) Grand Marnier
    4 oz. (¹/₂ cup) fresh lemon juice
    2 tablespoons superfine sugar
    6 drops Angostura bitters
    2 quarts (about 8 cups) pineapple
        juice
    hard ice cubes
Garnish: orange twists

Method: Mix everythng together in a
    punchbowl, taking care to dissolve
    the sugar. Serve on the rocks, and
    garnish with orange twists.

West Indian Rum Punch

An intimidating list of ingredients, but actually very simple to make and a real crowd-please
Koko Canu is a coconut rum from Jamaica, if you don't have it, use Malibu instead.

This drink should be prepared 4–6 hours before serving so everything can
marinate together.

Serves 18

Glass: 18 old-fashioned glasses
Ingredients: 10 black peppercorns
               8 oz. (1 cup) Morgan Spice rum
               16 oz. (2 cups) Bacardi 8 year old rum
               8 oz. (1 cup) fresh lemon juice
               5 oz. ($^2/_3$ cup) Koko Kanu
               1 vanilla bean, split lengthwise
               10 drops Angostura bitters
               4 tablespoons ($^3/_4$ cup) orange sherbet
               4 tablespoons superfine sugar
               2 quarts pineapple juice
               1 quart freshly squeezed orange juice
               4 ripe mangoes, peeled, pitted and pureed,
                 or 2 canned mangoes blended with the
                 canned syrup
               hard ice cubes
Garnish: lemon, orange, and lime slices, passionfruit,
               guava or any exotic fruit

Method: Gently crack a few of the peppercorns. Mix
               everything together thoroughly in a large
               punchbowl and leave in the refrigerator. Stir
               again, and serve on the rocks, and garnish with
               your chosen fruits.

Pimm's Royale

Pimm's is the classic drink of the English summer—in other words, usually consumed under the flap of a sodden marquee while rain lashes the cricket pitch. Originally made with 6 different liquors, now only the No.1 (a gin base) and No.6 (a vodka base) survive.

Serves 24

Glass: 24 highball glasses

Ingredients: 10 oz. (1¼ cups) gin (preferably
Bombay Sapphire)
2 bottles of Pimm's No. 1 Cup
1 carton of fresh strawberries, quartered
1 carton of fresh raspberries
1 carton of fresh blackberries
1 carton of fresh blueberries (optional)
1 large cucumber, sliced
1 small bunch of tarragon, chopped
6 large scoops of lemon or orange sherbet
3 tablespoons superfine sugar
champagne, prosecco, or you can use
ginger ale or ginger beer (to top up)
hard ice cubes

Garnish: mint leaves

Method: Mix everything except the champagne (or
other fizz) together in a large punchbowl, ladle
on the rocks into glasses, and top up with the
fizz and garnish with mint.

Rare blackened beef with pesto

The thin ends of tenderloins are cheaper than, but just as tender as, the rest of the tenderloin. Tenderloin of venison would work just as well.

4 beef tenderloins ends—about 7 ounces each—trimmed
1 tablespoon freshly milled black pepper
2 teaspoons coarse sea salt or kosher salt
1/2 cup plum sauce (or apricot jam, warmed)
7 ounces (a scant cup) basil pesto

Dry the meat with paper towels, then season liberally with black pepper and salt. Spread the beef lightly and evenly with plum sauce, then heat a stovetop grill or dry frying pan until smoking.

Sear the beef on all sides until it blackens—the sugar in the plum sauce helps the process—then rub the fillets liberally with pesto and let cool for 30 minutes.

To serve, slice the tenderloins fairly thinly and arrange on a wooden board or plate.

Seared sesame tuna with wasabi yogurt dip

This Japanese-inspired dish features wasabi, the fiercely hot green paste usually found on sushi and sahimi. Buy it in tubes, or buy the powder and make it yourself.

2 small loins blue-fin tuna, about 14 ounces each
1 cup sesame seeds
2/3 cup plain yogurt
2 tablespoons wasabi paste
few drops of sesame oil
1 teaspoon crushed garlic
coarse sea salt or kosher salt and black pepper

Season the tuna loins with salt and pepper, then press into the sesame seeds, making sure they are evenly coated.

In a hot nonstick skillet, gently color the tuna on all sides: this will take about 3 minutes. Leave at room temperature to cool.

Mix the yogurt, wasabi, sesame oil, and garlic together. Just before serving, fold in a pinch of coarse sea salt to add a little crunch.

To serve, slice the tuna fairly thinly and arrange on a board or plate next to a bowl of the wasabi yogurt.

Crostini

Crostini can be made from any good-quality bread: slice a French stick thinly, spread the slices on oven trays, drizzle with olive oil and bake in a 300°F oven until crisp and starting to brown (about 15 minutes), or slice ciabatta and broil it. Crunchy toppings work better on softer crostini; squishy toppings are more suited to crisp bases.

Onion, anchovy, & black olive

A miniature version of *pissaladière*, the famous onion tart from Nice. Anchovies are optional.

4 medium onions, peeled and thinly sliced in
  half rings
2 tablespoons olive oil
1 tablespoon fresh thyme, chopped
10 anchovy fillets, halved lengthwise
olive oil
10 black olives
sea salt and black pepper

In a heavy saucepan, heat the olive oil, add the onions, and gently cook until soft and almost all the liquid has evaporated (about 45 minutes). The onions should just be starting to brown. Stir in the thyme, season with salt and pepper, and leave to cool.

When cool, spread the onion mixture onto the crostini, then garnish with the anchovy strips in crosses, and top with olive halves.

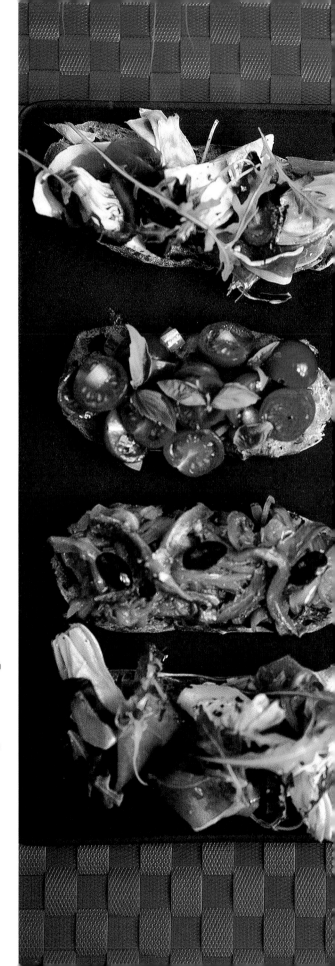

Prosciutto & artichoke

Best on toasted ciabatta: roasted red bell peppers can be bought in jars if you don't want to roast and skin them yourself.

¹/₂ cup tapenade (black olive paste)
3 baby artichokes, quartered
10 thin slices of prosciutto
wild arugula, to garnish
2 red bell peppers, broiled, skinned and cut into strips
olive oil

Spread the crostini with tapenade, top each with an artichoke quarter and a slice of prosciutto, then garnish with a few leaves of arugula and strips of red bell pepper. Drizzle with olive oil and serve.

Cherry tomato & basil

The marinating time is important here: the flavors and textures need a little time to meld together, but leave it too long and it will become too soggy.

18 ounces cherry tomatoes, cut in halves (about 3–3¹/₂ cups)
1 medium-size red onion, finely chopped
handful of basil leaves, shredded (reserve a few sprigs for garnish)
3 tablespoons olive oil
1 tablespoon lemon juice
1 teaspoon sugar
sea salt and black pepper

Mix everything together in a bowl, leave to marinate for 10 minutes, then spoon the mixture onto the crostini. Garnish with basil sprigs and serve.

Baked new potatoes with caviar & cream cheese

An extravagant but classic combination of warm, nutty potatoes, cool cream cheese, and the world's priciest eggs. Superb with frozen vodka martinis.

25–30 new potatoes
3 tablespoons olive oil
7 ounces (a scant cup) cream cheese
1 tablespoon lemon juice
tabasco, to taste
3 tablespoons chives, chopped
2$\frac{1}{2}$ ounces Beluga caviar (Avruga or
  salmon eggs—keta—are cheaper!)
coarse sea salt or kosher salt and
  black pepper
fresh parsley

Preheat the oven to 350°F.
Roll the potatoes in oil, sprinkle with salt, and bake them for 30 minutes, or until cooked. Set them aside in a warm place. Mix the cream cheese with the lemon juice and a dash of tabasco, season with salt and pepper, and stir in the chives. Cut a lengthwise slit in each potato, squeeze them to open, spoon a little cream cheese into each, top with caviar, and serve with a few parsley leaves on top.

Broiled asparagus with San Daniele ham

This can be made with any good air-cured ham; Italian prosciutto or Spanish serrano ham would work just as well.

20 spears of large asparagus
    (2 bunches)
2 tablespoons olive oil
juice and grated zest of 1 lemon
20 thin slices of San Daniele ham
sea salt and black pepper

Trim the asparagus, using a potato peeler to pare any tough stalks. Cook them in boiling, salted water for about 4 minutes: they should be crunchy and bright green.

Refresh the asparagus in cold water (iced, if possible) and dry them with paper towels. On a heatproof dish, roll the spears in the oil until well coated, then put under a hot broiler until they start to brown.

Remove them from the grill, add the lemon juice and zest, season with salt and pepper, and let cool.

When cool, wrap each spear in a slice of ham and serve.

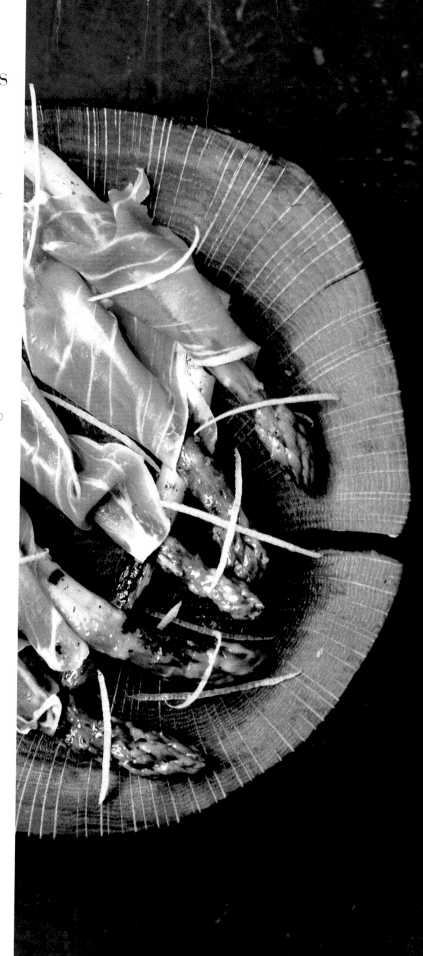

Crispy calamari with sweet chili sauce

Very addictive. Thai sweet chili sauce can be found in Oriental grocers and most supermarkets.

11 ounces cleaned baby calamari (squid), cut in half lengthwise
1 egg, lightly beaten
1 cup flour
1 teaspoon paprika
pinch of turmeric
1 teaspoon dried garlic flakes
pinch of cayenne pepper
2 teaspoons crushed black pepper
1 teaspoon coarse sea salt or kosher salt
1 quart sunflower oil
$1/2$ cup Thai sweet chili sauce
2 lemons, cut into wedges

Heat the oil to 350°F.

Coat the calamari in the egg, then drain to remove any excess. Mix all the dry ingredients together, toss the calamari in the seasoned flour, shaking off any surplus, and immediately fry until crisp and golden. Drain briefly on scrunched-up paper towels, and serve with a pot of chili sauce and lemon wedges.

walnut & stilton on endive spoons

5 ounces (about 1–1¼ cups) Stilton cheese, at room temperature
1½ tablespoons ruby port
1 cup chopped walnuts
3 heads of Belgian endive

Mash the Stilton and the port together with a fork and then fold in the chopped nuts.

Trim the roots of the Belgian endive heads, peel off the outer leaves, and discard, then drop the smaller, more tightly curled, inner leaves straight into a bowl of iced water.

Just before serving, arrange the endive "spoons" on a serving plate and put a teaspoon of the cheese, port, and nut mixture into each.